THE GREAT PYRAMID OF GIZA

HISTORY AND SPECULATION

James Bonwick

DOVER PUBLICATIONS, INC.
Mineola, New York

Bibliographical Note

This Dover edition, first published in 2002, is an unabridged republication of the work published under the title *Pyramid Facts and Fancies* by C. Kegan Paul & Co., London, in 1877.

Library of Congress Cataloging-in-Publication Data

Bonwick, James, 1817-1906.
    The Great Pyramid of Giza : history and speculation / James Bonwick.
        p. cm.
    Originally published: Pyramid facts and fancies : London : C. Kegan Paul , 1877.
    ISBN 0-486-42521-5 (pbk.)
    I. Great Pyramid (Egypt) I. Bonwick, James, 1817-1906. Pyramid facts and fancies. II. Title.

DT63 .B58 2002
932—dc21
                                                                            2002031303

Manufactured in the United States of America
Dover Publications, Inc., 31 East 2nd Street, Mineola, N.Y. 11501

PREFACE.

LONG interested as I had been in the Great Pyramid, the reading of recent pyramid literature in the free and sunny land of Australia quickened my desire to explore the building itself. A sojourn by the Nile, and subsequent study, led me to use my pen.

With so many books on Egypt already published, the only apology for my authorship is that no small work of condensed information upon pyramids has yet appeared.

To Prof. Piazzi Smyth belongs the honour of popularising the pyramid. Although failing to receive his theories, I respect his learning, reverence his motives, and am grateful for his labours. The French *savans* have been particularly interested in the pyramids, and have written so well as to become leading authorities.

The question of " Why was it built ? " has been here answered in nearly fifty different reported teachings from the rocky tomb. The divergence of opinion, while exciting a smile, illustrates the marvellous suggestiveness of the grand old edifice. The writer has no special ideas of his own to propound, but simply claims the merit of collecting intelligence for those whose time and opportunities will not warrant research.

A second work, as a necessary sequel to this, is in course of preparation. It will treat of "The Religion and Learning of the Ancient Egyptians." The symbolism of faith 6000 years ago cannot be unimportant to thoughtful persons now. The investigation of opinions existing at so remote a period may throw a light upon some views entertained in this day.

JAMES BONWICK.

Vale of Health, Hampstead, London,
        Aug. 28, 1877.

CONTENTS.

THE GREAT PYRAMID OF GIZA

HISTORY AND SPECULATION

WHAT IS THE GREAT PYRAMID?

EVERY one knows that the Great Pyramid has a square base and four triangular faces or sides, though not coming quite to a point at the top. Julius Solinus tells the world that "the pyramids are sharp-pointed towers in Egypt, exceeding all height which may be made by man." Ammianus Marcellinus echoes the same idea, saying, "the pyramids are towers erected altogether exceeding the height which may be made by man. In the bottom they are broadest, ending in sharp points at the top, which figure is, therefore, by geometricians called pyramidal." Propertius talked of their leading up to the stars.

While astonishing the ancients by its vast dimensions, the pyramid failed to excite much interest further in the minds of Greek and Roman writers. Some moderns are hardly astonished at it any way. Major Furlong merely calculates that it would now cost a million of pounds to build. M. Grobert, artillery officer under Bonaparte in Egypt, could not understand the fuss a few *savans* made about it. In his official report, he says, " Travellers have not entertained their readers about these pyramids. Their construction is rude and not very remarkable." Denon, who brought out, under Napoleon Bonaparte's patronage, the most magnificent work ever published on Egypt, was just sufficiently interested in the subject to acknowledge in his book, " We had only two hours to be at the pyramids."

Yet there are others who look upon the edifice as an echo of the Past. Every stone in the fabric has a weird look. The very outline seems to melt into the blue sky against which it reposes. On it, around it, and within it, the spiritual eye sees forms not now of earth. The ear is supernaturally quickened, and the heart pulses in sympathy with the men that were, and *are*. It is not the object of undefined dread, but of nameless soul attraction. To such enthusiasts the pyramid is alive; and they wait anxiously for expected revelations from it.

Those there have been, and still are, who regard that building as suggesting what it did to the Cambridge Christian Advocate, Mr. Hardwick :—"There if ever," says he, " we may hope to find the master-clue which is to guide us through the intricacies of primæval history, reveal afresh the hopes and fears which then were struggling in the human bosom, and resolve for us, it may be, many an arduous problem which concerns the origin, the early wanderings, and the final destiny of man."

For the present we have to dismiss romance and sentiment, and discuss the material question of the pyramid itself.

Strong as it is—the embodiment of strength—it is not everlasting. The elements may prove to be kinder than man. The almost cloudless skies of Egypt have smiled upon the ruins of the old land, as if cherishing the remains of what the destroying hand of man has spared. As contending sects in the primitive days of Christendom not only destroyed life, but the books of the opposite party, so rising dynasties of Egypt have sought revenge in the destruction of edifices erected by their adver- saries. Every change of religion has meant the mutilation of art symbols. The god dethroned spiritually beheld his very name removed from monuments.

It has been the habit to abuse the Turk for the ruin of ruins in Egypt. History does not substantiate the charge. The cultured Semitic race, the Saracens, are more open to the reproof. Turkish pashas have ruled since Western European travellers visited the Nile ; and not until the days of Mehemet Ali, of the European Albanian race, were these devastations known to any great extent. Mr. Gliddon declares that " until 1820 little injury had been done to the ruins." And this Vandalism has followed the presumed law of progress. The crushing of these glorious trophies of ancient civilisation has been in accordance with *Western Ideas.* Money was to be made. Money *must* be made. Money *can* be made by the breaking up of temples, and the using of their stones for sugar factories. And the progressive and much-extolled pasha broke up the temples and raised the sugar-houses.

In the sad lament of Mr. Gliddon, and his appeal to the *really* civilised for moral help against the barbarian, we read that three temples went to build the the factory of Esné, a part of Dendera temple for a saltpetre factory, the temple of Abydos for a bridge, the temple of Latou for a quay, and that the very chambers of the Nilometer were invaded. The temple of Syene then disappeared. The sixty-six steps which remained of the noble staircase of Elephantine were then missed. The foot of the great pyramid was a quarry for this Albanian utilitarian.

" Twenty years ago," said Mr. Gliddon in 1842, that neighbourhood " abounded in legends and tablets, supplying many vacuums in history ; *scarcely one remains.*"

The very pyramid itself stood in danger.   Mehemet Ali, in 1835, proposed to level it, for the sake of the blocks of stone. He only desisted from the undertaking on learning that it would be *cheaper* to quarry in the hill nearer Cairo.   An Arab, about the year 1100, bitterly lamented that " vile and unhappy men " had broken some of the stones of the pyramids, making, as he expressed it, " all see baseness and their sordid cupidity." M. Rénan may well thus cry out in alarm, " The work of Cheops runs now greater dangers than it has encountered for 6000 years ! "

A donkey ride of half an hour, or less, from that palace of comfort, " Shepheard's Hotel," brings one to the Nile bank at Old Cairo, Fostat, or Babylon.   Tradition says that the great Sesostris, whoever he was, brought captives from Babylon to settle there, or build the city.   It is a little beyond the interesting suburb of Boulaq, where the indefatigable and intelligent Mariette Bey has established his wonderful Egyptian Museum, till better quarters, long since promised, can be provided.

Cairo is one of the most delightful of residences, with a climate most enjoyable and healthful during the greater part of the year.   In spite of certain oriental squalor, clinging to oriental romances everywhere, it is a city of palaces and luxury. The European element has long dominated in its architecture and customs, though these are mostly French, as they are Italian in Alexandria.   Money can there procure every Parisian indulgence, and gratify every sensual desire.   The place is fast becoming popular with the English, who are more admired by the natives than other foreigners, because reputed more liberal in payment and more true to promise. Again and again has the writer heard the wish expressed that the English, and not the Khedive, ruled in the land.

Egypt under the English would recover its lost dominion. In India we have learned, *at last*, and to some appreciable extent, how to govern native races. The Turks in 400 years made small progress in the work. We have had but 200 years to learn the lesson, and have, according to some, made little advance. While condemning the Turk for despising the simple fellah of Egypt, the wily Greek, and the stolid Bulgarian, it is not for us to throw the stone while our Christian and educated countrymen in India call high-class Brahmins and other refined Hindoos by the contemptuous name of *Niggers*. It marks no more conciliatory policy.

Perhaps there is not a people anywhere more hopeful than the Egyptian. He is industrious, he loves the soil, he is patient, he is teachable, he is intelligent, and he is grateful for kindness. More than all, he has the blood of a noble ancestry. He is the offspring of a wonderful, though by-gone, civilisation. The oppression of foreigners for 2500 years has failed to crush his spirit, which seems as merry, buoyant, and free as the 5000 years old pictures display it to have been.

Professedly Mahometan, but never bigoted, they accepted the faith of Mahomet when conquered by Saracens from Arabia, as they submitted to bow to the Cross when commanded by Christian authorities. Passive obedience has been the distinguishing trait of the Egyptians from the earliest of times. Who can tell what changes for the better will come from the government of the energetic, self-willed, self-impressing, progressive Englishman ?

What a future for Africa to contemplate, should Egypt be our colony in the north, as the Cape in the south ?

But dismounting from the Pegasus of imagination, let us look at the pyramid in the most prosaic light.

It is of stone,—granite, marble, and limestone. The granite and marble are for the lining of passages and chambers. The main structure is of nummulitic limestone. This is generally called of Eocene tertiary age. There was an ancient period when a vast deep sea received an immense deposit, during untold thousands, or hundreds of thousands of years. It consisted of sandy *débris* of older rocks, with limestone concretions ; life, coralline and molluscous, existed in those warm waters. Gathering lime homes of various kinds, the animals took them to their graves in the oozy mud, and Time bound the whole as stone, and brought up the sea bottom to be a home for new-born men, from the pillars of Hercules to beyond the Indus. The empires of Babylon, Persia, Greece, Rome, of the Saracen, the Turk, the Moor, the Crusader, and the Pope have rested on this rock of history. The Babe of Bethlehem slept on it ; the pyramid of Gizeh was built of it.

The fossil life of the stone is marvellous, millions of tenements of beings are therein crowded to a cubic inch or so. Some of the larger concretions puzzled Herodotus. He settled it that they were the petrified date-stones of the workmen. He was equally right in his testimony that outside was a record of the expenditure of 1,600 talents for onions, &c., provided for the workmen. But both stories are susceptible of another interpretation. The granite, doubtless, comes from Elephantine and Syene on the Upper Nile ; as the alabaster from the Khalíl mountains, towards the Red Sea. The pyramid stones contain

0·95 carbonate of lime, 0·04 of alumina, and ·01 of oxide of iron. The Libyan hill on which the building stands is of that stone.

THE TRENCH.

In front of the pyramid is a singular trench, which seems to have escaped the observation of most travellers. Dr. Richardson, in 1816, first drew attention to it, saying, " There is a broad deep trench cut in the rock at the middle of the east front of the large pyramid, and running parallel with it. It is rather broader than a carriage road ; it descends toward the middle from each end, and resembles a carriage entrance to and from a pond. It is half full of sand, and is entered on the east side by a channel like a canal for the conveyance of water." He adds, " I am disposed to consider this is the channel by which the water of the Nile entered the·pyramid."

Mr. Agnew describes two trenches, north and south, and both parallel to the pyramid. He notices a third hollow, pointing to the causeway, and extending foɪ 198 feet. The other two were equal to it in length. Sir Edmund Beckett, in his valuable architectural work of 1876, speaks of trenches in the rock of the pyramid at an angle of 51° 50′ ; as he says, " apparently as models for the slopes on so large a scale as to avoid the risk of error." He thinks the men would find out the slope of the face, " and work stones by a template, setting them by a longer template or level with a plumbline to it."

THE CAUSEWAY.

Herodotus has a long story about the causeway, or raised road, by which stones, ready prepared, as in the case of the

Jerusalem temple, could be brought from the river to the site ; the base level being 140 feet above the upper cubit of the Nilometer at Rouda, or Rhodda, that is, about 130 feet above the valley of the Nile. This was said to have occupied ten years in the construction, and to have been faced or cased with stone, and adorned with hieroglyphics. It was five stadia long. What was a stadium? Some say 600 feet ; a French authority gives 610 feet ; Mr. Agnew says 603. This would make it over 3,000 feet long.

Diodorus wrote that it had disappeared in his day. It is only another proof of Greek inaccuracy. Professing to see, he gave only what he heard. Mr. John Greaves, Oxford Professor of Astronomy in 1637, believed the Greek historian, and did not look; contenting himself with, "there is nothing now remaining." Norden, the Dane, was there just a hundred years after, and noticed what he called the *bridge;* "There remains still a sufficiently considerable part of that admirable bridge to form a just idea of its whole structure, and of the use they made of it. There are likewise at the end of the third pyramid some remains of another bridge."

Pococke saw and described its ruins. An earlier foreigner gives an account of the remnant of this *causeway*, which he traced toward the Nile for 1,500 feet, when it was lost in the alluvium. But while he, too, observed traces of one leading to the third pyramid, he says nothing of one to the second. Richardson, when noting it, deemed that it was the road constructed by Saladin when he stripped the outer covering of the pyramid for his buildings in Cairo. Modern authorities conclude that it may be traced E.N.E. of the pyramid for 1,200 feet. Agnew expresses this opinion :—"I believe this great causeway led up to the eastern side of the great pyramid, and terminated in front, at 159 feet from the base, or at the eastern range of the circle describable about the base."

HOW IT WAS BUILT.

One reputed architect has informed the world that the whole was constructed of *pisé.* Water, by elaborate machinery, was led up to the required heights to mix with the sand, &c., to set in blocks of the needed size, and formed themselves tier by tier in the moulds. Mr. Perring thought scaffoldings were employed. Sir Gardner Wilkinson refers to the cutting away of the projecting angles, when they "smoothed the face of them to a flat inclined surface as they descended." This will meet the difficulty of its being finished downward.

Herodotus, the enigmatical historian, rather than the simple one, had before given this story. Dr. Lepsius, the German scholar, has his way of looking at it. "At the commencement of each reign," says he, "the rock-chamber destined for the monarch's grave was excavated, and one course of masonry erected upon it. If the king died in the first year of his reign, a casing was put upon it, and a pyramid formed; but if the king did not die, another course of stone was added above, and two of the same height and thickness on each side; thus, in process of time, the building assumed the form of a series of regular steps. These were cased over with stones, all the angles filled up, and stones placed for steps. Then, as Herodotus long ago informed us, the pyramid was finished from the top downwards, by all the edges being cut away, and a perfect triangle left."

Mr. Melville, the mystic, author of *Veritas,* has his view

of the transaction; saying, " Herodotus tells us the pyramids were ·finished downwards, and unquestionably they were. Books, learned books, as the writers fancy, have lately been published to explain this passage. Large blocks of stone have been supposed to have been lifted to their places, and then cut as required, and the *débris* thrown to the base. Oh, folly ! "

This is the story of the Greek :—" Having finished the first tier, they elevated the stones to the second by the aid of machinery constructed of short pieces of wood; from the second, by a similar machine, they were raised to the third, and so on to the summit. Thus there were as many machines as there were courses in the structure of the pyramids, though there might have been only one, which, being easily manageable, could be raised from one layer to the next in succession ; both modes were mentioned to me, and I know not which of them deserves most credit."

Sir H. James, of the Ordnance Department, thinks the working rule of construction was by two poles, one horizontal, ten feet long, and the other vertical, of nine feet ; as, " the inclination of each edge of the pyramid is what engineers call ten to nine." But Sir Edmund Beckett, as an architect, demurs ; remarking, " I do not at all agree with him that the builders worked by any such inconvenient rule as that—carrying up diagonally, slanting standards at the corners, and making the courses ' lineable by eye with them, however easy it may sound theoretically."

THE STEPS.

He who has once been hauled up by the three muscular, good-tempered, but .bakshish-loving *so-called* Arabs, but really

Egyptian fellahs, will not forget the steps. The ascent is by the north-east angle, where the stones are sufficiently knocked about to give a better tread.

Herodotus wrote nearly 2300 years ago :—"This pyramid was built in the form of steps." He adds that some call them *little altars*. When he tells us that one of these stones is thirty feet, we stare. He may mean cubic feet, as he calls the least of them that size. M. Grobert declares they vary from 1 foot 5 inches to 4 feet in length. He noticed a gradation. The first tier gave him an average of 3 feet 10½ inches ; the second, 3 feet 6½ inches ; the third, 3 feet 1½ inch ; then, 2 feet 11 inches ; 2 feet 8 inches ; 2 feet 3 inches. Mr. Perring, the accurate surveyor, gives the average of these courses at from 2 feet 2 inches to 4 feet 10 inches. About the largest stone is one 9 feet long and 6½ broad. Mr. Fergusson the architect has the average at 30 inches. The stones diminish as they approach the top.

One authority gives an elevation of 223 inches for the fifth course of masonry ; 869 for the twenty-fifth ; 1686 for the fiftieth ; 3052 for the hundredth ; and 5830 for the total vertical height. The Queen's chamber is said to be on the twenty-fifth course ; and the King's on the fiftieth course.

The number of steps has been a most unnecessary puzzle. Pococke, there in 1743, notes the difference from 207, Greaves's number, to 260, the number of Albert Lewenstein. But he goes on to say, " as Mallet, who also was very exact, counted 208, it is possible the number of the steps is 207 or 208, though I counted them 212." Thevenot, in 1655, made 208 ; Denon, in 1799, 208 ; while Lewenstein, or Lewenstainius found 260 ; Vausleb, in 1664, 255 ; Sandys, in 1610, 255. Bellonius got 250 ;

Lucas, 243; Johannes Helfricus, 230; and Grimino, 210. Siccard, in 1711, counted 220 ; Davidson, in 1763, 206 ; Beckett, 210 ; Grobert, in 1798, 205, with three crumbled ones, or 208. Fergusson has the number 203 ; while M. Dufeu has 202, the last two being in the centre of the upper platform. Prosper Alpinus, in 1591, could only count 125. The majority give 208.

The mortar, or cement, varies according to the work. Where used for passages or casing, it was of pure lime. But Perring, to whom we are so indebted for his work in 1837, found the ordinary mortar to be an odd mixture of pounded bricks, gravel, crushed granite chippings, and Nile mud. Sometimes it proved nothing but a simple grout, or liquid mortar, of sand and gravel only.

One architectural estimate of the time to rear the pyramid is as follows : allowing fifteen miles for carriage, and 300 days a year of ten hours a day for labour, the time for quarrying, elevating, and finishing would be 164 years. Herodotus, whose words need sometimes an interpreter, talks of 100,000 men and twenty years; that is, we may say, 10,000 men, as many as could work at it, for 200 years.

SIZE.

According to Perring, the original quantity of masonry was 89,000,000 of cubic feet, or 6,848,000 tons. As far as is known, the passages and chambers make but one-sixteen-hundredth part of the block. He states the present base is 12 acres, 3 roods, 3 poles; the former, with the casing, was 13 acres, 1 rood, 22 poles. The Egyptians had a great dislike to visitors prying about the place, particularly with a measure in their hands. A sheik once drew M. Grobert aside, and said, " It is useless

to give yourself so much trouble, there is no silver down in
there ; I swear it by Allah and my faith."

The height of the pyramid has been widely estimated.
Herodotus made it equal to the length. Bryant, in 1807,
wrote : "It seems at first to have been 500 feet in perpendicular
height." Thevenot gave 520 ; Greaves, in his "Pyramido-
graphia," 499 ; Perring, 450¼ ; Vausleb, 662 ; Perry, 687 ;
Lucas, 729 ; Niebuhr, 440 ; Gemelli, 520 ; Denon, 448. In
the last-named, the French architect employed to measure in
1799, was M. Le Père, aided by Colonel Coutelle, of the
Engineers. Fergusson states the present height to be 456, and
Colonel Howard Vyse, 450¾. The inclined height, says the
last authority, is 568¼. The vertical height, says M. Dufeu,
was never greater than it is now.

The base is practically a square. Herodotus gave the length
eight plethra or 800 feet, the same as the height. But that
height must have been the side of the triangle up. Tran-
scribers may cause authors to err. Thus, he is said to have
declared the third pyramid "wanting 20 feet on each side of
three plethra." It should have read *plus* twenty. Diodorus
appears to make the size 700 by 600 feet ; Strabo, 652 by
600 ; Thevenot, 704 by 682. Pliny gave the size, 708 ;
Grobert, 745⅔ ; Perring, 746 now, but once 764 ; Colonel
Howard Vyse accepts Perring's calculation. Sir Edmund
Beckett speaks of a difference of 4 feet in 761 "between the
measure made by highly competent persons." He deems the
761 of Sir H. James as "the best measure to adopt." This
includes the casing stones at the base. The Royal Engineers,
on their return from the Sinai survey, got these results : east side,
9,129·5 inches ; north, 9,127·5 inches ; west, 9121 inches ;

south, 9,140·5 ; yielding an average of 760¾ feet. Mr. Piazzi
Smyth has chosen a mean calculation of 763·81 feet.

The corner socket was found in 1797. The French dug down
through the rubbish at the north-east angle. This *encastrement*
or large hollow socket worked in the rocks, yet quite uninjured,
received the corner stone. It is an irregular square, three and
a half metres by three. At the north-west corner the other socket
has been discovered. The measure between, 232·747 metres, or
763·63 feet, was the base line. But Colonel Vyse's grand
discovery, in 1837, of a couple of the casing stones on the
parent rock, enabled us to get the more modern estimate of
correctness, 764 feet. These marble blocks were of exquisite
workmanship and truth of outline.

The angle of inclination in these two casing stones was first
given at 51° 50′. Prof. Piazzi Smyth, assuming it 51° 51′ 14·3″,
and the base line 763·81, obtained as the result for the perpendicular height 486·2567.

The orientation, or eastward aspect, is nearly perfect ; offering
a great contrast to the edifices of Thebes, &c., where the face is
any way. In fact Mr. Fergusson goes so far as to say that the
builders of Thebes had "no notion of orientation." It is not
5′ out of the line ; Mr. Piazzi Smyth makes the error but
4′ 35″. An earthquake, it has been conjectured, may have even
caused this slight error. The angles of the sockets of the great
pyramid have been given at 0, for south-east, + ·1 for north-east,
+ 1 for south-west, and + 0·636 for north-west.

THE CASING OR COVERING.

Upon this subject, as upon about all subjects connected with
the pyramid, there has been a difference of opinion. While

some maintain it was absolutely covered with a marble, or *satin*, dress, and others that it was but partially concealed by this stone drapery, not a few hold that it has never been covered at all.

A *pavement* has, however, been noted at the foot. Though not rectangular, it is finely fitted, for all the pyramid work was beautifully done. It is not of uniform width round, varying from twelve to thirty-three feet. The thickness is a foot and three quarters. Under the pavement was seen a fissure, filled up with small stones.

Herodotus, our earliest authority, claims an entire marble covering for the pyramid, and states that the stones were skilfully connected, none being less than thirty feet, the top being first completed. This was declared to have been carried off by Salah-è-Deen, the Saladin of history, of the time of our Richard the First, for the adornment of his new city and citadel at Cairo. The magnificent Mosque of Hassan, one of the most remarkably beautiful religious edifices in the world, so impressive of pious sentiment, is said to have been constructed of this marble.

M. Jomard recognised the story of the *revêtement* or covering, and Grobert discussed the retention by notches or grooves. Maillet, a very frequent visitor, writing in 1692, believed the building had been closed ; saying, " I concluded that the pyramid had been really covered and lined." Pococke, in 1743, has thus named the subject :—" It is thought that this, as well as the other pyramids, was cased with a finer stone on the outside, because it is said that not only the mortar has been seen in which the stones were fixed, but also some pieces of white marble sticking to the mortar, which they think were left on their taking away the stone for some other use." Still, the worthy traveller was puzzled to think how such smooth covering could be clambered over; for, he adds, " Pliny mentions a very extraordinary thing with regard to these pyramids, and that is, that some men were so very adroit that they could go up to the top of them."

The second pyramid has certainly a cap of marble left, and that has been ascended by the athletic and nimble Gizeh Arabs. The third pyramid was covered with granite, so toughly put together that Melic-aliziz, in 1196, could not succeed in stealing it. But Mehemet Ali did get some of the marble casing of a Dashoor pyramid. Belzoni found part of the coat of the smallest of the Gizeh structures beneath the rubbish.

The stones found by Col. Howard Vyse were both casing ones. The joints were as thin as paper. The block was of trapezoid form; the base being 8 feet 3 inches, the perpendicular side 4 feet 11 inches; the top 4 feet 3 inches; and the slanting side, 6 feet 3 inches. The material came from the quarry of Mokattan, beyond Cairo, and is commonly known as *swine-stone*, or *stink-stone*, from the odour proceeding from this marble when struck; but few fossils have been detected. Perring observed the smell at the time of discovery. Broken in fragments, for relics, where are now these stones ?

Count Caviglia, the pyramid enthusiast, picked up pieces of the casing on the eastern side in the *débris*. Mr. Agnew found sundry pieces among broken stones on the western sides. "The discovery of these portions of the lubricated face of the great pyramid," he observes, "must remove any doubt of its having been finished, could such doubt ever exist." He regards the thing as settled, that the passages were effectually blocked, and the outside was covered; it was intended that the pyramid should be *closed for ever.*

Sir Edmund Beckett points out another object served by the casing. "The lowest course of casing stones," he remarks, "had a square or upright plinth as high as the pavement, which was laid for a considerable width all round the building, and such was the precision of the building, that this pavement was varied in thickness at the rate of about an inch in 100 feet, to make it absolutely level, which the rock was not."

But M. Dufeu doubts the story of the *revêtement.* He could not deny that Colonel Vyse had found two casing stones, though these were, said he, "a *débris* of a valence put round it to guard it from the ravages of time," and not ascending any height. He quotes from M. Letronne, that "the first, perhaps also the second, step of the lining formed a sort of valence, like the pedestals of obelisks." He knew that his countryman, Jomard, had pronounced with Herodotus, but for all that, Dufeu declares, "in spite of the report of Herodotus, the historians of antiquity, and the opinion of the remarkable *savant* (Jomard) just cited, the great pyramid *has never been covered.*"

He is not wanting in arguments. Such a casing would destroy the teaching of the 202 steps, so important to the learned Frenchman's scientific theory, that is elsewhere described. It would have been absurd for Saladin to pull off such a casing, when he could get the same kind of stone at one-tenth the distance from Cairo. Before he could use such marble prisms, so uniform in size, a vast amount of cutting would be required for actual use, and a great waste be incurred. To save trouble and carriage, such alteration would have doubtless been made on the spot, and "Where," cries he, "do you detect the *débris* of the marble?" The mere hauling down of the slabs would induce fractures, leaving fragments, which are not now to be discovered. Most of the *débris* of the pyramid is at the southern and western sides, most exposed to weather, and consists of particles of the stone steps, brought down by wind and rain, besides sand blown up from the desert. Furthermore, he naturally asked why the supposed Saracenic spoiler, in his anxiety for marble casing, did not take it from the more convenient little pyramids, but pass them by to attack the more formidable building?

THE TOP.

It is a glorious view from the upper platform over the level but continuous garden of the Nile. One looks down upon the plain where Bonaparte's squares repelled the charge of the Mameluke horsemen, and which glorious feat was witnessed, not by forty centuries, but by sixty. The mysterious desert and the Libyan hills stretch northward, southward, and westward. The site of Memphis and the marvellous old pyramids of Saqqarah are before one. There lie the tombs of the sacred bulls; and around the pyramid are the graves of kings, nobles, priests, and ladies of the Ancient Empire, 5000, 6000, or more, years ago. Quiet thoughts on the pyramid are suggestive ones.

When Thevenot was there he counted " twelve lovely large stones." Greaves, the astronomer, wrote:—" The top of this pyramid is covered, not with one or three massy stones, as some have imagined, but nine, besides two which are wanting at the angles." Another describes it " surrounded with thirteen great stones, two of which do not now appear."

The top has been generally estimated at 30 feet. Dr. Richardson has this statement :—" Arrived at the summit we found it ample and spacious ; a square, from 25 feet to 30 feet a side, consisting of long square blocks of stone, with the upper surface coarse and uneven, as are the usual surfaces of stones in the courses of a building. We perceived a thin cement of lime be_ tween the different courses of stones, but there was *no appearance of any cement having been placed upon the upper surface of the highest course.*" The conclusion was that it had never been higher. Mr. Agnew said :—"The platform was not intended to form part of the pyramidal portion of the monument." But Dufeu and others regard the platform as the real top, which was never covered, though it may have had a column or *cippe* to serve as an imaginary apex.

The Rev. T. Gabb, 1808, who had no doubt of its being originally pointed, as were all the other pyramids, was a little troubled to account for this being stripped of the top while others retained theirs in safety. "Nor do I doubt," quoth he, "but the apex was severed from it by the impetuosity of the waters (*at the Flood*) while in their unabated rapidity, and thus left the flat, which has furnished various conjectures." Others that retained their caps, when the Flood carried off the top of the great pyramid, were, thinks he, "erected nearer to the time of the Deluge, it may be even a thousand years after the great one."

Having now taken a survey of the exterior, the consultation of authorities concerning the interior will next engage attention.

Although some reference elsewhere has been made to the *name* of the building, it may not be out of place to say something here upon

THE NAME.

Murtadi, as an Arab, thinks the Arabic *birba*, plural *barabi*, is probably corrupted into *pyramis*. But Pococke and Sacy call *birba* a *temple*. Thevenot says the Turks call it *Pharaon Daglary*, and the Arabs *Dgebel Pharaon*, meaning *Pharaoh's hills*. Abenesi and others thought the first syllable of the word was only the masculine article in Egyptian. The word *el Harm* or *ancient*, is an Arabic derivation. Abdullatiff writes :—" Galen speaks in one place of the pyramids, and he derives their name from a word which signifies the decrepit state of old age." According to Galen himself, " we call him who is in the third epoch of old age *haram*, and those who love to search etymology say this word, which is given him, is derived from that of the pyramids (*ahram*), into which they ought soon to take their place."

On this the Professor of Arabic in Paris, 130 years ago, M. Vattier, had this observation :—" The pyramids are expressed in the Arabian tongue by two names, *Birba*, which I have used in several places, and *Haram*. Haram, in the Arabian, signifies an old structure." Macrizi speaks of *Ahram*, the pyramid. D'Herbelot observes, " *Ehram* or *Eheram*, Arabic plural of *Herem*, which signifies *old age*, this plural, joined to the article, makes *Alehram*, and signifies, in particular, the pyramids of Egypt, because of their great antiquity." Michaelis would give the same. *Ah'ram*, according to others, is the local name now given to the pyramids ; *El-Haram* is said to be a corruption of *Pi-Haram*.

Silvestre de Sacy says :—" This name (*Haram*) signifies the *holy place, the edifice consecrated in a particular manner, it may be to some divinity, or some religious usage.* It is very possible that the Egyptians might have written 'HRAM, without any vowel after the aspirated consonant, as they write even now 'HRA, *face,* &c., and it is not surprising that the Greeks may have supposed that aspiration too hard for them." He sees, however, some objection :—" The first is that the root HRM is not found in modern Egyptian. That objection does not appear strong to me. We know but very imperfectly the Coptic language, and above all the dialect of Said."

Jablonski takes up Pliny's ray definition of the obelisk, saying —" The Egyptians then gave the name of pyramids to the obelisks, because they had a sort of resemblance to the rays of the sun ; afterwards they carried that name to more considerable edifices, which one properly names *pyramids,* because that, nowithstanding that their distinction was different, they preserved some relation to the figure of the solar rays." Elsewhere he notices the Coptic words *pirá-mona, splendour of the sun.* Lacroze gets *pi-re-mi* as the *splendour of the sun.* Ammien Marcellion, or Marcellinus, says :—" It got the name because it ends in a cone, imitating in that the fire." But as De Sacy properly adds, " That only offers the first part of the word, *pyr.*"

Adler and Rossi find it in *pi-rama, height,* or a raised monument. Silvestre de Sacy, citing this opinion, tells us that " This etymology possesses faith and simplicity, and the most strikingly sensible application to the pyramids." Wahl sees the Coptic root *ramas, rich.* Wilkins reads *pouro, king,* and *mici, birth,* because intended for royal families. Lacroze has for interpretation, " the inhabitant or possessor of the elevation." Kircher finds a meaning in *hero ;* adding, " the *piromes* were then statues of the kings and priests, which were raised as a witness of the

superiority of their strength, and of their heroic actions." Dufeu
has *pi-re-mit*, to mean the tenth part of measures or numbers.
Volney gives the definition of *cave of the dead.* "In ancient
Greek," says he, "the *u* was pronounced *oo ;* we should therefore say *pooramis. Pooramis* is not Greek, but Egyptian."
He thinks *pour* or *bour* is *prison* or *sepulchre,* and *amit* is *of the
dead.* Others, from the Greek *puros,* wheat, and *metron,* measure, may have imagined the story of Joseph's granaries. As
a Coptic word it may mean a measure of ten. Prof. Smyth has
the authority of the editor of the *Hebrew Christian Witness*
for "considering the word *Matzaybhah* in Isa. xix. 19 to
mean a *pyramid.*" The same word is translated *pillar* there,
and in Gen. xxviii. 19.

THE OPENING.

Whether absolutely cased or not, the pyramid was practically
shut up, according to popular account, until about the year
830, when the Caliph Mamoun found an opening. For this story
we are indebted to Arabian sources, which are slightly doubtful.
The truth is generally somewhere, though nearly overwhelmed
by imaginative details.

One of the well-known versions is about Al-Mamoun, Caliph
of Babylon, gaining access to the interior. When he got to the
king's chamber, we are informed that he saw there a hollow
stone (the Sarcophagus), in which lay the statue of a man. But
the statue inclosed a body, whose breastplate of gold was
brilliantly set with jewels. A sword of inestimable value lay
upon the corpse. At the head shone, with the light of day, a
carbuncle as large as an egg. We have also a tale about one
Melec-Alaziz-Othman-ben-Yousouf, who made so desperate an

attempt to break into the third pyramid, that eight months were spent in the work of destruction. It would be difficult to determine if they succeeded in moving a single stone.

Then we are informed by one Arab that Caliph Abdal-la Mamoun, the opener of the great pyramid, was the son of Haroun-al Raschid, of the "Arabian Nights Entertainments," and the contemporary of Charlemagne.

That which appears probable is, that the Saracens began on the north side, as reported by tradition to have been that by which the Romans had once entered ; but that, while the latter, and any other previous visitors, had been content with the descending passage to the subterranean chamber, the former were the first to penetrate by the gallery to the king's chamber. One of the Arab stories of the opening is thus related by Ibn Abd Al Hokm :—

" After that Al-Mamon the caliph entered Egypt, and saw the pyramids. He desired to know what was written within, and therefore would have them opened. They told him it could not possibly be done. He replied, ' I will have it certainly done.' And that hole was opened for him, which stands open to this day, with fire and vinegar. Two smiths prepared and sharpened the iron and engines which they forced in ; and there was a great expense in the opening of it. The thickness of the wall was found to be 20 cubits ; and when they came to the end of the wall behind the place they had dug, there was a pot of green emeralds. In it were a thousand dinars very weighty ; every dinar was an ounce of our ounces. They wondered at it, but knew not the meaning of it. Then Al-Mamon said, ' Cast up the accounts. How much has been spent in making the entrance ? ' They cast it up, and lo ! it was the same sum which they found; it neither exceeded, nor was defective."

On the other hand, Macrizi declares that the Caliph Mamoun was only forty-nine days in Egypt altogether; a time utterly short of that required by the Arab stories. Denys, the old traveller of the twelfth century, would surely have mentioned some facts of the wonders of the interior, had they reached him at Cairo. He does narrate something; for, said he, "We looked in at an opening which was made in one of the edifices, and which is 50 cubits deep." His idea of a cubit may be seen from his giving the height of the pyramid 250 cubits, and the base 500. De Sacy is justified in saying that "he could not have neglected to make mention of a discovery so important, and which would have refuted completely the fable of the granaries of Joseph;" an opinion cherished at that period. He concludes that "the opening of the Great Pyramid is more ancient than the journey of Mamoun in Egypt."

Whoever forced an entrance failed to strike the right spot, though a way to the Descending Passage was obtained by the removal of obstructing stones. The present entrance is 47½ feet above the base, and by the fifteenth or sixteenth step. One may ride up to it on the vast mass of rubbish in front. It is there the visitor is met by the sheik and his tribe, when a treaty is made as to charges for attendants. The standing tariff is about four shillings for each man, and two men are the minimum for a person, while a larger douceur is expected by the venerable chief.

When Sandys was there, in 1610, the difficulties of an entrance were greater than at present. It is now as it then was, "full of rubbidge." But we have no stories in this day of men going in, and coming up again some thirty miles off.

His experience at the entrance is thus detailed :—"In this our Janizaries discharged their harquebuses, lest some shuld haue skulkt within to haue done us mischiefe, and guarded the mouth whilst we entred, for feare of the wilde Arabs."

THE PASSAGES.

Although the entrance was supposed to have been made by a Mahometan Caliph, this singular passage occurs in Strabo : " On high, as it were, in the midst between the sides, there is a stone which may be removed, which being taken out there is a *shelving entrance* leading to the tomb." He is careful in another place to add, " This entrance was kept secret." When Greaves came to this shelving passage, in 1637, there was no ready access. " We hire Moors," wrote he, " to open the passage, and to remove the sand, before we can enter into the pyramid." The travellers are now too numerous, and their *bakshish* is too acceptable, to have the sand difficulty ; though they have, like Bèlon, of Mans, in 1554, to enter it with candles, and go " after the manner of serpents."

It is no easy walking or groping, though one has not to contend, as Greaves had, " with many large and ugly bats, a foot long." The descent is pretty steep, and the way is both narrow and low. The width is 41 or 42 inches, and the height 47 inches. After proceeding downward for 63 feet, the groper changes his posture for the *Ascending Passage*, at a similar slope for 124 feet ; but which is about the same size as the other, though Jomard has it 43 inches wide, and Caviglia, 42. At its summit there are two passages :—one, the horizontal, 109 feet long, 41 inches wide, 43 or 44 high, leads to the Queen's

Chamber; but the other, still ascending in the slope, is the celebrated Grand Gallery. A yellowish-looking marble lines the passages. The term *Syringe,* of Greek derivation, has been used by foreigners to express levels or narrow subterranean passages. The passage to the south from the Subterranean Chamber is 52 feet long, 2½ broad, 2½ high.

The angle of the passage has originated much discussion. While M. Jomard makes it 25° 55', Col. Howard Vyse and Perring have 26° 41'. Prof. Smyth calls it 26° 18'. As the angle of the inclination of the pyramid to the horizon is about 51° 50', Mr. Fergusson, the architectural authority, concluded that the angle of the passage was intended to have been about one half of this. The half of 51° 50' would be 25° 55'. He further says, " The angles are not the same in any two pyramids, though erected within a few years of one another, and, in the twenty that were measured by Col. Vyse, they vary from 22° 35' to 34° 5'." While some observers of the Great Pyramid have jumped to the idea that the angle of the side was 40°, others ran it up to 60°. The double of Mr. Smyth's 26° 18' would give 52° 36'.

Why this particular angle of 26° or 26° 18' should have been adopted for the passages has aroused much interest. The astronomical arguments of Mr. Piazzi Smyth and others will be considered in another part of this work. But that inclination is called by Sir Henry James " the angle of repose." Mr. Fergusson writes, " The angle of the passage was the limit of rest at which heavy bodies could be moved, while obtaining the necessary strength where they opened at the outside, and the necessary difficulty for protection inside, without trenching on impossibility." It was said that the blocking-stones of the passage, hereafter to be described, could be easily slid along the floor at that angle. But, then, it has been shrewdly remarked that the descending passage, along which these portcullis stones were not required to slide, is at the same angle as the ascending one.

Mr. Agnew, for reasons mentioned elsewhere, concludes that the intention of the builders was to have it 26° 33′ 54″. "Other passages," he thinks, "with the same inclination, may probably exist, leading in a zigzag direction to upper rooms on the levels of the other inscribed squares of the figure."

A remarkable incident in passage history is noted by the able French traveller, Maillet, French Consul, who spent sixteen years in Egypt, made forty visits thither, and was the earliest of the modern pyramid enthusiasts, being quoted with high respect by our traveller Pococke in 1743. M. Maillet speaks thus : "a discovery which I have made in the upper part of the passage of 118 feet, which leads there. It is that the stones which compose it are *split across in all the length of the passage*." He conjectures that an earthquake caused it.

Greaves made what he supposed a discovery. "On the east side of this room (Queen's Chamber)," said he, "in the middle of it, there seems to have been a passage leading to some other place. Whether this way the priests went into the hollow of the huge Sphinx, as Strabo and Pliny term it, or into any other private retirement, I cannot determine ; and it may be, too, this served for no such purpose, but rather as a *theca* or *nichio*, as the Italians speak, wherein some idol might be placed."

The *Descending Entrance-Passage* proceeds in one straight course toward the Subterranean Chamber, and is, according to Mr. Perring, 320 feet 10 inches long; originally, when the

entrance was in order, it must have been about 343. When the
second and successful attempt was made to force an entrance,
the Caliph's workmen struck this passage near its junction with
the first Ascending Passage, meeting with the granite portcullis
difficulty there. While the real entrance is 48 feet from the
base, the Saracens, in 820, made a hole about 20 feet above the
base, driving horizontally, and thus met the bottom of the
Descending Passage. Owing to the loss of 23 feet from the roof
of the entrance, the Descending Passage is now but 63 feet to
the junction with the Ascending one.

The *Upper or Ascending Passage*, at the angle 26°.18', or, more
accurately it is said, 26° 17' 38", is 125 feet long. Perring
puts it at 124 feet 4 inches long, 3 feet 11 inches broad, and 3
feet 5½ inches high. One gropes along that with the same
difficulty as in the first. Mr. Waynman Dixon, C. E., a
recent and careful observer, discovered that the masonry of
this Ascending Passage is strengthened at intervals by the
"insertion of collars, or huge plates of stone, through the middle
of each of which the passage is made to pass by a perforation of
its own size."

Arrived at a landing or platform, two passages appear. One
is the Grand Gallery, a continuation of the ascending slope, and
at the same angle, though not of the like height, width, and
length. The other is the *Horizontal Passage*, nearly as long as
the Ascending, and leading directly to the Queen's Chamber.
Perring has the following measurement of it :—from the lower
end of the Gallery to the low passage, 16 feet 7 inches ; thence
to the step, 92 feet ; from the step to the Queen's Chamber, 17
feet 11 inches ; or a total length of 109 feet 11 inches. The
breadth he calculated at 3 feet 5½ inches ; the height, at 3 feet

10 inches before the step in the passage, and 5 feet 8 inches after that spot.

The passage to the Subterranean Chamber is direct from the entrance to where it strikes the bottom of the well, when it turns horizontal, instead of the angle 26°, for several feet. After passing through the Subterranean Room, another passage is seen at the farther end, going horizontally to the south, or opposite side from the entrance. It is 52 feet 9 inches long, 2 feet 7 inches wide, and only 2 feet 5 inches high. M. Jomard, in 1799, was confused, he tells us, with "the passages, oblique, horizontal, sharply-bended, of different dimensions."

THE WELL.

This is off from the landing-place of the Ascending Passage, from which one ascends the Grand Gallery.

Pliny describes "a well of 86 cubits in depth," which communicated with the waters of the Nile. Herodotus had spoken of the Nile being turned in to where the monarch's tomb lay, and the well was supposed to lead down to it. Bèlon, in 1554, spoke of it as that "which is now, as it were, filled with stones." Thevenot, a little after, wrote thus : "A well 123 feet deep, but such as have descended into it found nothing but sand, and a multitude of bats, which are ready to eat a man up."

Our Sandys, 1610, like Thevenot, was content to stay at the top. "Others have written," says he, "that at the bottom there is a spacious pit, 80 and 6 cubits deep, filled at the overflow by concealed conduits ; and, in the midst, a little island, and on that a tomb containing the body of Cheops, King of Egypt, and the builder of this Pyramis, which with the truth hath a greater affinity. For since I have been told by one out of his own experience that, in the uttermost depth, there is a large square place (though without water) into which he was led by another entry opening to the south, known but to few (that now open being shut by some order), and entered at this place where we feared to descend."

M. de Breves, who wrote in 1605, has this addition : " At the bottom of this descent is a space to the left hand, from which another descent proceeds, which goes very much lower under the pyramid, but the entrance of it is walled up." Greaves, 1637, indicates the position thus : " This narrow passage lieth level, not rising with an acclivity, as doth the pavement below and roof above of both these galleries. At the end of it is the well." He goes on to say, " The diameter of it exceeds three feet, the sides are lined with white marble, and the descent into it is by fastening the hands and feet in little open spaces, cut in the sides within, opposite, and answerable to one another, in a perpendicular." He did not descend, only remarking, " By my measure, sounding it with a line, it conteines twenty feet in depth." M. Maillet, 1692, thought the well was " to facilitate the retreat of the workmen, after they had distributed, for the closing of the interior passages, all the stones which were shut up in the Gallery, each according to its destination." Richardson, in 1816, reminds his readers that it " is now found to be a secret passage of 150 feet long, and about 3 feet wide, furnished with niches on three sides for the hands and feet, by which to ascend to the upper chambers in the pyramid."

Count Caviglia, to whom the pyramid-admiring public are so much indebted, made an exploration with Mr. Consul Salt, in 1817. He found the central chamber named by Sandys. The

shaft, as Bunsen terms it, descends perpendicularly for 26 feet.
It then slants down 32½ feet to the *Grotto*, which chamber is in
a bed of gravel in the midst of the Gizeh rock, and is 17 feet in
extent.   Another slope of 133 feet leads down to the known
bottom, which is dry.   Mr. Perring makes the total length 191½
feet.   French authorities make it 207¾ feet, of which 145½ are
in the solid rock.   At a depth of 148¼ feet below the base of
the pyramid, it would be, it is said, 10 feet below high water of
the Nile, and 16 above low water.   From the bottom of the
well it is 24 feet to the Subterranean Chamber.

THE GALLERY.

This is, next to the King's Chamber, the most interesting part
of the Great Pyramid, and its measurements have given plenty
of employment to theorists.   We must acknowledge, with grati-
tude, the zeal with which Prof. Piazzi Smyth has sought for information concerning it.

The old English astronomer, John Greaves, was much im-
pressed by the Gallery : " Not inferiour," says he, " either in
respect to the curiosity of art, or richness of materials, to the
most sumptuous and magnificent buildings."   He may well
characterize it as " the labour of an exquisite hand."   He noticed
the grand roof of seven overlapping courses of stone, and the
two stone banks, ramps, or benches, running both sides the full
length of the Gallery.   He calls them " banks of sleek and
polished stone ; each of these hath one foot 717 of 1000 parts
of a foot in breadth, and as much in depth."   The path between
he found to be $3\frac{485}{1000}$ feet wide, giving $6\frac{870}{1000}$ feet for the
full breadth.   In alluding to the ramps, Sir E. Beckett says :—

"The channel clearly was for something heavy to slide down between them," alluding to the stones to block up the passages.

The shrewd Mr. Greaves took note of the perpendicular cutting in the ramps, each cutting opposite to one on the other ramp; "intended," thought he, "no question, for some other end than ornament." Sir H. James, as well as the architect Beckett, wrote of them, alluding to the blocking design by means of them, thinking that the blocking stones were kept at the foot of the deep step at the top of the Gallery, and slid down over planks. "The portcullis stones," he says, "are 2 cubits wide, and 48 inches high, to fit their ultimate place exactly; and the channel between the ramps is just over 2 cubits, and the ramps themselves just under a cubit, leaving about 7 inches on each side as clearance for the stones to slide down easily." Perring makes the ramps 2 feet high, $20\frac{1}{2}$ inches broad, and $41\frac{1}{2}$ inches passage between the ramps. The holes are 26 in number on one ramp and 28 on the other, two being beyond. The cutting is vertical, and not at right angles to the Gallery.

The step-holes in the floor are alluded to in Montfaucon, from M. le Brun, of the seventeenth century, who observed :— "The stone bench $2\frac{1}{2}$ feet high, and proportionately broad, which they hold fast by in going up, to which the holes that are made in the pavements at almost every step contribute not a little, though coarsely made, and without observing exactly the distances between them; without these holes for to take footing, it would be impossible to go up to the top, nor is it without a great deal of difficulty that one can get there with this assistance." These cuttings, for travellers' convenience, are, of course, roughly hewn. Pococke mentioned them in 1743.

As to the length of the gallery, Greaves wrote :—"From the well below to this partition above is an hundred, fifty and foure feet." Among the estimated lengths, in inches, are the following :—Richardson, 1440; Jomard, 1461; Maillet, 1488; Coutelle, 1595; Caviglia, 1824; Greaves, 1848; and Thevenot, 1944. The careful Perring measured 150 feet 10 inches to the step, and 5 feet 2 inches thence to the passages to King's Chamber, making it 156 feet, or 1872 inches. This step at the head of the Gallery is 7½ feet high. An Arab received the writer off from the top of it in his arms.

The height of the Gallery may be considered 27 feet 6 inches, or 330 inches. It has been called 270 inches by Shaw, 300 by Maillet, 312 by Greaves, 336 by Vyse, 360 by Caviglia, and 350 by Piazzi Smyth, who thus gets seven times the ordinary height of the other passages. The angle of ascent is 26° with Greaves, 27° with Wilkinson and Coutelle, 26° 18′ by Vyse, and 26° 17′ 35″ by a subsequent calculator.

The stair-like roof, as Mr. Fergusson says, is 28 feet high, and assumes the form of inverted stairs, till it contracts so much at the top that no pressure can hurt it. M. Grobert rather derides the plan, saying, " If the Egyptians had been more learned in the art of construction, they could have covered by a *voûte en berceau* the ascending Gallery, which would have occasioned less work, less expense, and more solidity." It is quite likely they knew better than the Frenchman what they wanted, and how best to accomplish their object. M. Maillet's interpretation is seen under the heading of " Blocked up." There are 36 inclined stones to form the roof.

THE QUEEN'S CHAMBER.

Mr. Greaves said, "Leaving the well, and going on straight upon a levell, the distance of fifteen feet, we entred another square passage. This leadeth into an arched vault, or little chamber; which, by reason it was of a grave-like smell, and halfe full of rubbage, occasioned my lesser stay. This chamber stands east and west, the length of it is lesse than twenty feet, the breadth about seventeen, and the height lesse than fifteen. The walls are entire, and plastered over with lime; the roofe is covered with large smooth stones, not lying flat, but shelving, and meeting above in a kind of Arch, or rather an Angle."

Norden, in 1737, saw it "half filled with stones." Maillet had before remarked the forcible entry, and that "stones broken, and drawn from that place, still fill now almost all the capacity of the chamber." He noticed the roof was "made like an ass's back." He refers to the niche on the east side, three feet in the wall, "and of the height of eight upon three feet," the space sufficient for the queen's coffin. Richardson, sixty years ago, spoke of it in the north-east corner, and like the queen's closet, or dressing-room. Both were empty, and not lined with granite. This niche is not in the middle of the wall. One describes it as 15 feet high, and two cubits broad, gradually contracted by short offsets, from 65 inches wide at the bottom to 25·3 at the top.

Two channels there looked like the air-holes of the other Chamber, but were sealed up. When broken through, the space was horizontal for 7 feet, and then turned north and south at the angle 32°. They might have been for acoustic purposes. Mr. Waynman Dixon tested them by smoke, which was not to be detected outside. A rounded granite ball, supposed a Mina

weight, being 8825 grains, was taken from the northern channel.
Some speak of the Chamber as seven-sided. From the base
of the pyramid to the floor of this room is 67 feet 4 inches.
The area is 18¾ by 17 feet. The height is from 14 feet 9 inches
to 20 feet 3 inches. The Queen's Chamber is more beneath the
top of the Gallery than under the King's Apartment.

THE KING'S CHAMBER.

The Gallery contracts suddenly at the upper end, and does
not lead at once into the King's Chamber. There is first a small
low passage, then the Ante-chamber, and another short passage.
There is a low granite doorway, and one has to creep beneath
the unfallen portcullis or "granite leaf;" another low doorway
must be passed before the Chamber is gained. The portcullis,
which was intended for closing purposes, is described as a flat
stone "found sticking up," which "had never been let down."
The distance, says Perring, to the King's Chamber, including
the portcullis' space, is 22 feet 1 inch. The height of the passage part is 3 feet 8 inches; the two passages comprehend an
extent together of about a dozen feet, five on one side and seven
on the other. The sides of the Ante-chamber and passages are of
granite.

The *Ante-chamber*, or *Anti-closet* of Mr. Greaves, is fitted on
each side with four grooves for the reception of portculli or flat
stones, to be let down to block up the way to the King's Room
from the Gallery. Mr. Smyth made the size 115 pyramid
inches. The height is about 14½ feet. As he writes, "On
either side are opposite sets of broad hollow grooves ; three being
very broad ones, and one moderately broad, the latter, though

a part of its height is occupied by a granite block or plate, which hangs suspended in it, and underneath which every one must pass."

Greaves wrote thus : "This inner Anti-closet is separated from the former by a stone of red speckled marble, which hangs into two mortices (like the leaf of a sluice) between two walls, more than three feet above the pavement, and wanting two of the roof. Out of this closet we enter another square hole, over which are five lines, cut parallel and perpendicular." A boss has been noticed upon this leaf or portcullis. Each groove has a semi-circular top. A French authority makes the whole side to be 9 feet 10 inches long ; the width of the groove filled by the portcullis is about 20 inches. Three portculli were thus pro-vided for. M. Jomard, nearly eighty years since, thought these three singular *travées* had no analogy with anything he knew. The height of the portcullis, according to Perring, is 12 feet 5 inches. Mr. Waynman Dixon found a bronze hook near there ; it may have belonged to some treasure-seeker of old.

Looking at the Ante-chamber, M. Maillet thought of the first invaders, and exclaimed, " How many difficulties would they not have had to surmount in order to conquer the King's Chamber ! It was," he added, "the last refuge of the architect." In his day the relics of the struggle were to be seen. He observed the fragments of the stones broken by the workmen, now removed to make the way smooth for the *bakshish* bestowing Englishmen. One great stone, 6 feet by 4, lay before him. His further remarks are noticed in the " Blocking " article.

In Aristotle we read : " Now, as with admiration we behold the tops of the pyramids, but that which is as much more under-ground opposite to it we are ignorant of ; I speak what I have received from the priests." Yet Strabo had heard of a *cell* being there.

The *King's Chamber* is, in spite of the spoliations, a beautiful granite-walled apartment. Noble slabs of granite, 20 feet high, and admirably joined, line the sides. The roof is flat. There is no furniture but the ever-mysterious *Coffer* or *Sarcophagus*. Pietro della Valle, in 1615, said, "The pyramid was, perhaps, constructed for several persons; but I have found no tomb in one or the other (chambers)." Sandys wrote admiringly of it, saying, "A goodly chamber twenty foote wide and forty in length; the rooffe of a maruelous height; and the stones so great, that eight floores it, eight rooffes it, eight flagge the ends, and sixteene the sides, all of well wrought Theban marble" (granite).

The story by Mr. Greaves, the Oxford Professor, is too important to omit. He passed through the *Anti-closet*, crept through "another square hole, over which are five lines cut parallel and perpendicular," and stood "at the north end of a very sumptuous and well-proportioned room." The rest of his account is as follows :—"This rich and spacious chamber, in which art may seem to have contended with nature, the curious work being not inferiour to the rich materials, stands as it were in the heart and centre of the pyramid, equidistant from all the sides, and almost in the midst between the basis and the top. The floor, the sides, the roof of it, are all made of vast but exquisite tables of Theban marble (granite). From the top of it descending to the bottome, there are six changes of stone. Of these, there are nine which cover the roofe; two of them are lesse by halfe in breadth then the rest, the one at the east end, the other at the west."

Again he writes: "From the top to the bottom of this chamber are six ranges of stone, all of which being respectively sized to an equal height, very gracefully, in one and the same altitude all round the room. The stones which cover this place are of a strange and stupendous length, like so many huge beams lying flat and traversing the room, and withal supporting that infinite mass and weight of the Pyramid above." He truly calls it "a glorious room."

He gives the length of the chamber $34\frac{380}{1000}$ feet; the breadth, $17\frac{190}{1000}$; the height, $19\frac{1}{2}$ feet. Perring reckoned it 34 feet 3 inches long, 17 feet 1 inch broad, and 19 feet 1 inch high. From the base of the pyramid to the floor of the chamber it is 138 feet 9 inches. It is beyond the centre, from the entrance side, by 16 feet 3 inches. While the temperature of the pit or well was found by Coutelle to be 25°, that of the chamber was 22°. He noticed, in 1799, a thick bed of dung on the floor. He speaks of an echo in the opening repeating six times. Dr. Richardson supposed that by removing one of the granite slabs at the side an access might be gained to other chambers.

The *Air-Chambers* of the chamber are two rectangular holes at the side; which, says Mariette Bey, "may be like the rectangular hole in the partition of the principal chapel of the tomb, or mastaba, which communicated to the deposit of images (of the departed), and before which, it is believed, prayers were said, and incense burnt." But though the very outlet has been found outside, the hole being closed showed that no air could reach the chamber. Sir E. Beckett thought they were " for the benefit of the mummy of the king, or the breathing of the undertakers and masons."

Norden said: "They appear to me vent holes to give air to

the chamber." Greaves thought them "receptacles for the burning of lamps." The north channel is 233 feet long, with an angle of 33°. One is 9 inches by 6, and the other 9 by 9. One passes to the north or right side of the pyramid, and the other to the south. Perring notes that they are 3 feet from the floor. One, 8 inches by 6, runs to the north 233 feet; the other southward, 174¼ feet long, 8⅞ inches broad, and 9⅛ inches high. The north channel bears the angle of 33° 42', and the south 45°.

THE SARCOPHAGUS OR COFFER.

This is the most interesting portion of the most interesting monument in the world. The suggestive views concerning it are stated under the heading of "Why was the Pyramid built?"

This lidless box or trough stands toward the further end of the King's Chamber, but rather to the right on entering. It is of porphyry stone, of extraordinary hardness and closeness of composition, ringing like phonolite when struck. In capacity it is, according to the corrections of Prof. Smyth, 77·806 inches long, 26·599 broad, and 34·298 deep; or a cubical measurement of 70,982·4 inches. The thickness of the sides is 6⅜ inches; and of the bottom, 7⁴⁄₉ inches. The outside length, says Bellonius, is 144 inches; Villamont, 102; Jomard, 90·592; Vyse, 90½; Caviglia, 90; Wilkinson, 88.

M. Jomard and others have asserted that it was too small for a sarcophagus. But, as Mr. Kenrick pointed out, it is 6½ feet long; and, as an average Egyptian was not above 5½ feet in height, there would be a foot space left for the cartonnage, or mummy case, &c. Prof. Greaves quaintly remarked, "A narrow space, yet large enough to conteine a most potent and dreadful

Monarch, being dead, to whom, living, all Ægypt was too streight and narrow a circuit."

The material has been called marble, granite, porphyry. They who see the association of the Pyramid with Scripture affirm that it is porphyry from Mount Sinai. The Syene granite is unlike it. Mr. Greaves was told by a Venetian, that he had seen at Sinai a similar stone to the sarcophagus, black and white, and red speckled. Similar porphyry is known in that neighbourhood. The quarries were worked at the period of pyramid building, as the cartouche inscriptions of King Khufu, the builder, have been discovered on the rocks near Wady Maghara.

As the vessel is too large to have been brought in after the formation of the intervening passages, it must have been lowered to its place before the roof was closed.

No lid was ever mentioned, although Bunsen declares he has "no doubt a king was entombed there." But Perring delineates the catchpin holes for a lid; and says: "There are not any remains of the lid, which was, however, fitted on in the same manner as those of the other pyramids." Maillet saw none in 1692; but he writes: "This chest had its covering, as one may remark by the fashion of its edges; but it has been broken in removing it, and there remain no vestiges of it." Jomard observes, "The lid, if there ever existed any, as that is very probable, has disappeared."

Prof. Smyth has these statements: "The western side of the coffer is, through almost its whole length, rather lower than the other three, and these have grooves inside, or the remains of grooves once cut into them, about an inch or two below their summits, and on a level with the western edge; in fact, to admit a sliding sarcophagus cover or lid; and there are the remains of three fixing pin holes on the western side, for fastening such cover into its place."

Bryant, the advocate of the Arkite theory a hundred years since, had no idea of a coffin lid. " It is indeed said," observed he, " that a stone coffin is still to be seen in the centre room of the chief pyramid ; and its shape and dimensions have been accurately taken. It is easy to give a name, and to assign a use, to anything which comes under our inspection; but the truth is not determined by our surmises. There is not an instance, I believe, upon record, of any Egyptian being entombed in this manner. The whole practice of the country seems to have been entirely different. I make no doubt but this *stone trough* was a reservoir for water, which, by means of the well, they drew from the Nile."

It is placed exactly north and south. The eastern side is double the distance of the western. The floor is perfectly level, and is $138\frac{3}{4}$ feet above the base of the Pyramid, which is said to be the same distance, $138\frac{3}{4}$ feet, above high water of the Nile. Behind the sarcophagus are traces of some excavation, eight feet by two.

The record of early visitors to this memorable and venerable object will be interesting to the reader.

The early Arabian authors are most positive about the box being used as a tomb. The most celebrated of these is Ibn Abd Al Hakm. He narrated the incidents connected with the breaking open of the pyramid, by orders of the Caliph Mamoon. Dr. Rieu, of the British Museum, a competent authority, tells us that " the statement relating to Al Mamoon's discovery could hardly rest on a better authority than that of Ibn Abd Al Hakm ; for not only was he a contemporary writer, having died at Old

Cairo, A. H. 269, that is, 38 years after Al Mamoon's death, but he is certainly quoted by later writers, as an historian of the highest authority."

Yet not only he, but, according to Col. Vyse, a number of other Arabian authors, allude to the discovery of a body with golden armour in the Sarcophagus of the King's Chamber. Al-Raisi says he saw the case from which the body had been taken standing at the Cairo palace-door, in the year A.H. 511; that is, in 1133. The same thing was observed by Abou Szalt and others. Dr. Sprenger adds, "The Arabian authors have given the same account of the pyramids, with little or no variation, for above a thousand years."

This is Ibn Abd Al Hakm's report: "Toward the top a chamber, with a hollow stone (the coffer), in which there was a statue like a man, and within it a man, upon whom was a breastplate of gold set with jewels; upon this breastplate was a sword of inestimable price, and at his head a carbuncle of the bigness of an egg, shining like the light of day; and upon him were *characters writ with a pen, which no man understood.*"

Bèlon, in 1554, described the chamber:—"Six steps long and four steps wide"—"in which," said he, "we found a coffer of black marble, made of a single piece, like a box,—which is without a lid." Thevenot, the other early French traveller, saw there "an empty tomb, that sounds like a bell, 3 feet 4 inches high, 3 feet 1 inch wide, and 7 feet 2 inches long. It is like porphyry, well polished, and very beautiful. It is thought to have been built by that Pharaoh that was drowned in the Red Sea." Sandys, in 1610, has a somewhat similar account:— "Athwhart the roome at the upper end there standeth a tombe; uncouered, empty, and all of one stone; breast high, seuen feete in length, & not foure in breadth, and sounding like a bell."

Norden afterwards described it as "a long urn, or, to speak more properly, a sarcophagus of stone, which has merely the figure of a parallelopiped, without any ornament besides. All that can be said of it is, that this piece is well hollowed out, and that it sounds like a bell when you strike it with a key." He dignifies the material by the name of "granite marble." Le Brun, of the 17th century, writes :—"This stone, which is above five inches thick, is extraordinary hard, and resembles porphyry. It is polished like glass."

Prof. Greaves, with his accurately divided ten feet rule, is so exact and truthful, that one turns with great satisfaction to his report :—

"Within this glorious roome (the King's Chamber), for so I may justly call it, as within some consecrated oratory, stands the monument of Cheops, or Chemmis, of one peece of marble, hollow within, uncovered at the top, and sounding like a bell." Quoting then from Diodorus—"'*Although* (saith hee) *these Kings intended these for their Sepulchers, yet it hapened that neither of them were buried there . . For the people being exasperated against them, by reason of the toilsomnesse of these works, and for their cruelty and oppression, threatened to teare in pieces their dead bodies, and with ignominy to throw them out of their Sepulchers, whereupon both of them, dying, commanded their friends privately to bury them in another place.'* This monument, in respect of the nature and quality of the stone, is of the same with which the whole roome is lined ; as, by breaking a little fragment of it, I plainly discovered, being a speckled kind of marble, with black and white and red spots, as it were equally mixed, which some writers call Thebaic marble, though I conceive it to be that sort of porphyry which Pliny calls *Leucostictos*. The figure of this tombe without is like an Altar, or, more nearly to expresse it, like two cubes finely set together, and hollowed within; it is cut smooth and plain, without any sculpture and ingraving, or any relevy and imbossements."

After stating that Bellonius made the length 12 feet, and De Breves 9 feet, he gives his own exterior measurement. The depth and breadth were 3 feet $3\frac{3}{4}$ inches. The hollow part within was, said he, $6\frac{488}{1000}$ feet on the west side, $2\frac{218}{1000}$ on the north, and $2\frac{860}{1000}$ in depth.

Maillet, for sixteen years French Consul in Egypt, whose accurate survey so deeply interested Mr. Pococke, our traveller, calls this "a box of granite marble." After speaking of its size, he says, "It has been so placed, from being shut in from above; and if it remains yet to our days in its entirety, it is because it cannot be drawn from the place it occupies without breaking, and the *débris* would be of no use. It is without doubt this chest which contained the body of the king, enclosed in two or three caskets of precious wood, following the custom which was practised with regard to the great."

It is most important to note that Maillet, at the close of the seventeenth century, with Norden and others of the eighteenth, speak of the Sarcophagus as *entire*. Not until Europeans, especially English and American ladies and gentlemen, began to stream thither, did the Vandalism of destruction commence. It was not sufficient to hew off masses from the exterior, but this precious monument, which no Turk had presumed to defile or injure, began to experience the usual fate of relics, at the hands of relic-worshippers and relic-thieves. Dr. Richardson, in 1816, was the first to observe the change. " A small fragment," said he, " has been broken off one of the corners."

With the exception of that small fragment, the noble coffer was safe sixty years ago. They who look upon it now, chipped and knocked about so cruelly, may well blush for Western civilisation. The writer himself was coolly asked by one of his Arab followers if he would like a piece broken off. With no one responsible for its preservation, and with the native expectation of a franc for a fractured piece, who can wonder at the gradual diminution, and ultimate total destruction, of this most wonderful and mystical box.

THE CHAMBERS OF CONSTRUCTION.

Immediately over the King's Chamber, and built so as to relieve it of pressure, are five chambers, called after Mr. Davison, the Duke of Wellington, Lord Nelson, Lady Arbuthnot, and Col. Campbell. The nearest was found by Mr. Davison, in 1763. Col. Vyse discovered the rest in 1837. A small hole, towards the ceiling at the upper end of the Grand Gallery, led Caviglia, by a forced passage, to the chamber above. The rooms are divided by granite, polished on the roof or upper surface, not the floor. The fifth, or Campbell's Chamber, has a roof of two sloping blocks. It has eight beautifully wrought stones. The passage leading to Davison's room is $24\frac{3}{4}$ feet long.

The sizes of these chambers, as ascertained by Mr. Perring, are pretty similar. All of them have smooth roofs and rough floors. From the floor of the King's Apartment to the top of the highest chamber of construction is $69\frac{1}{4}$ feet. Davison's Chamber is 38 feet 4 inches by 17 feet 1 inch, and from 2 feet 6 inches to 3 feet 6 inches in height, the floor being so uneven. Wellington has the three measurements of 38 feet 6 inches, 17 feet 2 inches, and 2 feet 2 to 3 feet 8 inches; Nelson, 38 feet 9 inches, 16 feet 8 inches, and 2 feet to 4 feet 10 inches; Arbuthnot, 37 feet 4 inches, 16 feet 4 inches, and 1 foot 4 inches to 4 feet 5 inches; Campbell, 37 feet 10 inches, 20 feet 6 inches, and 5 feet 10 inches to 8 feet 7 inches high.

A piece of iron, found in the masonry by Col. Howard Vyse, is now in the British Museum. It may have been brought from the iron mines of the Wady Maghara, near Sinai.

INSCRIPTIONS OF THE PYRAMID.

Herodotus was told a tale which he told again, about an account being written on the pyramid of the cost of provisions to the workmen. For radishes, garlic, and onions, the expenditure had been 1600 talents of silver. There is a double meaning under these words and the numbers. Somebody has suggested that degrees, minutes, and seconds may have been intended. The Greek, if he understood, shed no light upon the subject, though he added, "If this were really the case, how much more was probably spent in iron tools, and in bread, and in clothing for the workmen!"

Vausleb, in 1673, wrote about the pyramids, "I saw upon some of them some hieroglyphic characters, but I had not time to write them out." Norden, the Dane, sixty years after him, failed to see anything of the sort, and was surprised. "If I conjecture," said he, "that the pyramids, even the latest, have been raised before they had the use of hieroglyphics, I do not assert it without foundation. Who can persuade himself that the Egyptians would have left such superb monuments without the least hieroglyphical inscription? they who were profuse of hieroglyphics upon all the edifices of any consideration."

This remark was followed up by Dr. Templeman, 1792, thus:— "Why might not the same thing have happened to other hieroglyphics that were originally inscribed on the pyramids? And, therefore, the argument is not conclusive to prove that the pyramids were antecedents to hieroglyphics. Herodotus mentions several inscriptions that he saw on the pyramids, but they have vanished long since." The worthy doctor might have known that the climate of Egypt is favourable to the preservation of monuments, and that the inscriptions are usually so deeply engraved upon almost ever-enduring stone, that little or no change can be detected after being in use for at least four or five thousand years.

Then this question seems to rest upon the casing question. Had the pyramid been covered with granite or marble, such inscriptions mentioned by Herodotus would have been upon it, and disappeared with the casing itself.

But why do we see no writing upon the pyramids which retain the casing? Richardson would not interpret the Greek historian literally. "The small part of the coating," he observes, "which remains on the second pyramid has no hieroglyphics. The larger pyramids at Aboukir, Sakkarah, and Dakschour, are all coated, but have no hieroglyphics; and I am humbly of opinion that the Pyramid of Cheops, or that of Mycerinus, had none either."

As the pyramid was to be but a tomb, the ancient Egyptians treated it as they did the Sepulchral Chamber of the ordinary

burial; they left it silent. It was in the upper chamber, open
to friends, that the hieroglyphics and pictures abounded, as it
was there religious service for the dead was often performed.
The temples which once, as it seems, stood in front of the
pyramids, and were used for the worship of the heroes of the
edifices, had, doubtless, their usual inscriptions and adornments.
The pyramid was closed, securely closed, and had no tale to tell
to passers-by.

At the same time, Herodotus is not alone in his story. It
must be allowed that no Roman and Greek historian mentions
the letters. But our Maundeville has something to say about
the supposed Granary of Joseph. He wrote thus in 1330 :—
"and aboven the Gerneres withouten, ben (are) many Scriptures
of dyverse languages."

Others about that time have similar narratives. In 1336,
Baldensel said he saw a number of inscriptions. There was one
in Latin, six lines in extent. Ludolf, the pilgrim, 550 years
ago, gave the world a copy of a Latin discourse on one of the
two larger pyramids. He distinctly relates the finding of Greek,
Latin, and "unknown character" inscriptions, and that upon
all the four sides. The Arab authors, who enter more into particulars, speak after the same fashion; so much so, that Lord
Lindsay exclaims, "All the early Arab writers bear witness to
the existence of these inscriptions." Abd'allatif, in the thirteenth century, added to this information. "These stones,"
said he, "are covered with writing in that ancient character, of
which no one now knows the value. These inscriptions are so
numerous that if one could copy upon paper those only which
may be seen upon the surface of these two pyramids one would
fill more than 6000 pages."

This is plain testimony from personal observation, and goes a long way in support of the theory of the casing. Still, Orientals have a vision far more acute than Europeans, and listen with less critical ears than ours.

At one time it was boldly avowed that no writing was to be seen within or without. But Colonel Howard Vyse, in 1837, found quite a number of hieroglyphics in the Chambers of Construction over the King's Chamber. These rooms were made simply to take the bearing off the roof of the royal apartment, and were not held too sacred for pollution. Perring, in his magnificent work, gives several plates of these inscriptions. He found them on the east and west ends of Wellington Chamber; the west of Nelson's, the south, west, and north sides of Arbuthnot's; and the east, west, north, and south sides of Campbell's. They are in red paint.

Among these were the quarry marks of King Khufu, or Cheops, such as we recognise in tombs. Two royal names are thus distinguished. One name is phonetic. The Baroness Minutoli, in her charming letters, relates that her husband, in 1826, saw over several doorways, in the Great Pyramid of Saqqarah, decided hieroglyphics; "not hitherto remarked," she truly said, "in the other pyramids." Dr. Lepsius saw the hieroglyphics over the doorways, and detected their extreme antiquity, older than the quarry marks of the Great Pyramid; for, says he, " The encircling line for the king's name is put after the letters expressing it, instead of round them; and a square, instead of oval, banner, or title, is employed." He was a German *savant*, not a Vandal, yet he cut off this precious writing and carried it away to Europe.

THE SUBTERRANEAN CHAMBER.

According to the theory of the pyramid being a tomb, this apartment would correspond to the Sepulchral Chamber at the termination of the pit or well attached to an ordinary Mastaba. In all pyramids, the coffin was put below the surface, as in all tombs. We have reason, therefore, to assume that the Great Pyramid was no exception to the practice, and that in this Subterranean Chamber, if anywhere, the corpse of the monarch would have been interred. The unfinished state of the apartment, and the absence of any signs of a tomb, do not invalidate the argument.

Ibn Abd Al Kohm, in his account of the opening of the pyramid, has this singular statement :—" Within they found a square well. In the square of it there were doors. Every door opened into a house (vault), in which there were dead bodies wrapped in linen."

When Caviglia forced his way to this chamber, sixty years ago, he discovered that some one had been there before him. On the blackened roof, he saw Greek and Roman characters inscribed. While Diodorus is silent, Herodotus declared, " Some secret vaults are hewn in the rock under the pyramid." But though the ancients managed to get into this chamber, " they did not seem," one says, " to have discovered the secret of the other chambers." Sir Edmund Beckett, who maintains that the box or trough in the King's Room was really the sarcophagus, considers that the approach to the Subterranean Chamber was made easy in order to mislead persons seeking for Cheop's tomb.

There are two ways of access : one by the pit or well, and

the other from the outer air by an inclined passage, the continuation of that descended in the first instance by all travellers. The
room is reached after 300 feet of regular descent, when the person finds he is 100 feet below the base of the pyramid, and under
the centre of it.

Dr. Richardson arrived there immediately after the discovery,
and has left this account of his adventures after leaving the
King's Chamber :—

"We retraced our steps, and reached the orifice that led us
from the entrance passage ; here we turned to the right, and kept
descending by the same smooth passage to survey the interesting discoveries of Captain Caviglia, in which he was liberally as-
sisted, in pecuniary matters, by Mr. Salt and Mr. Briggs. Having
descended about 200 feet, we came to the bottom of the well,
which terminates on a level with the bottom of the passage, and
seems merely a niche in its side. Having descended for about 23
feet further, we came to the end of the inclined passage ; from
this point we could see distinctly up into the open air ; it looks
directly towards the north, and at night the Polar star is distinctly seen. The passage, proceeding onward from this, is cut
out in the rock, and is quite horizontal for 28 feet ; it ends
in a large chamber, 66 feet long and 27 wide, and between 12
and 14 feet high, and which is supposed to be exactly under
the centre of the pyramid. The chamber does not appear to
have been completely finished ; there is a bench of the solid rock
still remaining at the west end of it, high on each side, and low
in the middle."

The workmen superintending the closing of the King's Chamber, Antechamber, Grand Gallery, and Ascending Passage, could,
after letting slip the apparatus which lowered the stones, descend

the well to the Subterranean Chamber. Then, having secured the well exit, to prevent the possibility of one discovering the ascent, they could easily retreat up the one slope of 300 feet to the entrance of the pyramid. All that then remained to be done was to block up the first Descending Passage, and secure the opening.

The chamber, by Perring's measure, is 46 by 27 feet. He estimated the roof to be 90 feet 8 inches from the base of the pyramid. It has a flat roof, but an irregular floor. The height may average 11½ feet. Richardson says of the passage leading to it, that it is "lined on all the four sides by finely-polished slabs of large-grained red granite of Assouan." That place is 500 miles off.

Many believe that other chambers and passages exist, to be reached from the Subterranean Chamber. Richardson has thought of this, saying, "The stones are remarkably well cut and well fitted to each other, and probably cover the orifices of other passages into other chambers in the pyramid. Those at present known are all on the west of this general passage; that is, in the north-west quarter of the pyramid."

After all, we fail to get any light upon the strange story by Herodotus, that Cheops was buried on an island below the pyramid, and that water from the Nile surrounded his tomb. Mr. Ramsey, the companion of Lord Lindsay there in 1837, writes: "It is a pity no one thinks of looking for any probable entrance to the chamber in which Herodotus says the king is buried, in a sarcophagus isolated from the rest by the water of the Nile, which enters and flows round it. The level of the Nile is 130 feet below the foundation; the angle of descent always used here is known."

Mr. Agnew has, as usual, something of weight to add upon

this question. " I believe," says he, " there must be, to the
Great Pyramid, another entrance, on a level with its base ; but,
perhaps, on the eastern side, if not on the northern. If, from
this point, the passages be found to descend at the same angle
as the other, it would touch the circumference of the larger or
outer circle, from whence a communication could be found leading directly below the centre of the pyramid. This point,—in
parts 331·3698, or about 159 feet below the pyramid base line,
—would be 15 feet above low water mark, and 9 or 10 feet
below high water of the Nile in these times. Here, if anywhere, will be found the chamber of the sarcophagus, resting on
the island round which the sacred water circulated ; "where
Cheops himself is said to lie." But whoever occupied this
central place of honour below-ground may not have been the
only sleeper beneath the mighty mass."

An attempt, in 1837, by sinking below the floor of the
chamber, revealed nothing of interest. The descent was 36 feet.
But, with Prof. Piazzi Smyth, we cannot but wonder that while
money can easily be found for almost any mad project, a few
thousands of pounds to explore the noblest and most suggestive
of monuments cannot be obtained.

THE BLOCKING-UP OF THE PYRAMID.

Assuredly one of the most wonderful of the wonderful stories
to be told of the pyramid is that a building of such constructive
design, so full of teaching in it, should have been carefully and
effectually closed after its completion. Here, apparently, the
wisdom of the Egyptians was at fault.

Strabo said that the entrance was kept secret in his day. No

Greek or Roman writer records anything of the interior, excepting floating traditions, or the reports of Egyptian priests to
Herodotus, &c.   Arab writers alone tell the tale of the forced
entrance, and they dwell upon the difficulties encountered.   Had
not the passages themselves, including the Grand Gallery, been
blocked up with huge stones, the Caliph would have had no
obstacle to surmount after once striking the first or Descending
Passage.

All writers admit the existence of the so-called PORTCULLIS.
This granite stone, prepared and fixed for descent at the proper
time, so as to bar a passage, is found in several positions of the
interior.   The one at the foot of the first passage was too formidable for the invaders, who cut through the softer stones
beneath, and so made a detour to gain the Ascending Passage,
rather than hew any longer at a granite block which they had,
in the course of their excavations, heard fall down, when they
had got nearly 100 feet from the entrance.

The Portcullis is about 8 to 10 feet each way, and weighing
from 50 to 70 tons.   Some one calls that at the bottom of the
Ascending Passage only 13 tons.   Perring says the lower end of
the upper passage was filled with granite blocks for 14 feet.
The Portcullis was of a rectangular form, held in suspension at
the side, but fitted, at a signal, to fall and block up the passage.

Fergusson informs us that "they generally slide in grooves in
the wall, to which they fit exactly."   Furthermore, he reports :—
"These were fitted into chambers *prepared during the construction* of the building, but raised into the upper parts, and, being
lowered after the body was deposited, closed the entrance."

Not only were these shapely stones of granite here and there
swung, as it were, ready for their destined work of concealment,

but it is now determined that the old builders had other arrangements by which this stoppage was effected.　Not content with
the giant Portcullis of granite, a large number of marble blocks
were prepared *in* the building, at the time of construction, and
not after the passages were formed, for the sole purpose of
being dropped, according to pre-determined plans, and so effectually, as it was thought, keeping the interior sacred from
the eye and foot of intrusion.

The men of Khufu little dreamed that hereafter the desert
tribes would bring the overwhelming force of a new and burning faith, the strength of an irresistless tide of conquest, which
should shiver to fragments the massive doorways of these secret
ways.

What proof is there of this blocking?

In our days, we pass along the passages, up the Grand Gallery,
and enter the Royal Chambers, without the presence of these
stony *impedimenta*.　When Norden was there, in 1732, he observed more than we can do now.　He recognised the blocking
of the first passage, saying, "It is there (at the bottom) we discover clearly the manner in which the first passage has been
closed up, by means of *three* rough pieces of oriental *marble*,
which join so well the sides of the passage that one has a difficulty to introduce within the joints the point of a knife."

Of course he naturally, though erroneously, supposed that
these huge stones were introduced *after* the passages were completed, and brought down one and up another of them.　In
this he was considerably puzzled.　"It is pretended," he says,
"that all these passages *have been closed and filled up with great
square stones* which had been introduced thither after the whole
work was finished.　This, at least, is certain, that the extremity

of the second passage has been stopped; for we *still see* two
great square pieces of marble, which cut off the communication
between this and the first passage. But, to say the truth, it is
not large enough at the entrance for a man easily to pass, and
still less for introducing so *great a quantity of large stones as
were necessary for stopping up the other passages.*"

Here we perceive that, 150 years ago, there was a very decided
belief in Egypt that *all* the passages had been thus closed with
large stones. Arab tradition records the immense trouble the
workmen had to burst through these, the mutinous spirit of the
men exposed to such toil and danger, and the increased determination of the sovereign to proceed, as he felt confident that
such vast ingenuity and labour expended in the blocking must
have been for the concealment of enormous treasure.

The Danish traveller was equally struck with the precautions
adopted to preserve the integrity of the King's Chamber, which
enclosed the sacred deposit of the coffer or sarcophagus. In the
antechamber to the king's apartment he reported an important
witness, saying, "It has on each side an incision made in the
stone, probably in order to introduce these stones which were
designed to close up the entrance of the chamber."

Caviglia could have told more had his attention been directed
to the point. But Perring, who alludes to the lower part of the
Ascending Passage being filled with granite blocks for 14 feet,
affirms his conviction of the probability that *all* the passages were
once so filled. Bunsen, too, held such an opinion.

But it is to M. Maillet we are most indebted for attention to
this interesting subject. His long-continued and frequent observations were collected by Mr. Pococke, in 1743, and given in
his huge folios of travels. Let us read the Frenchman's report.

It must have been regarded as authentic when our countryman wrote, " For the particulars of the inside of the pyramid, I refer to Maillet's account, which I have added at the latter end of this volume." But Pococke's book is not the only source of this information.

M. Maillet tries to account for the presence of stones three or four feet thick employed to block up the passages.

The visitor would be ready to acknowledge the force of his remark that " In the whole length of this passage they (the invading workmen of the Caliph) were obliged to use violent means to break the stones with which it was filled up ; which so defaced all the sides of the passages that, whereas it was at first square, it became almost round." We can even now almost detect here and there the smooth marble surface of the original side. "All the passages," he continues, "have been filled up; the Gallery had a magazine of stones necessary for the closing of these passages." These must have been placed there before the finishing, as it was "impossible, after the pyramid was finished, to make any stone enter into that Gallery of a thickness necessary to block the passage from the inside and outside."

He perceived "the design of the architect in that long groove which exists at the bottom of the Gallery." The first passage, called by Maillet the *canal extérieur*, was once "filled with proportioned stones," subsequently drawn with much labour. Then "the stone which responded to the angle of the two passages was raised." Two hundred and twenty feet were thus blocked up.

Recalling the hard struggle of the Saracens to enter, he says : " They had reason to think that, besides the great number of stones which filled up this passage, there might be some other

place above, where there might be still more stones ready to
slide down and fill up this passage as fast as they endeavoured
to clear it. This was an additional labour which the architect
had proposed for those who should attempt to penetrate into the
centre of the pyramid." The workmen, after breaking through
the successive stony barriers, felt that at any moment some portcullis might drop down from some secret retreat and enclose
them alive in the tomb.

His observations upon the blocking of the Gallery are of
especial interest. He calls attention to the two raised steps,
benches, or ramps. "I have already mentioned," says Maillet,
"that in the benches on each side of the passage in the Gallery,
which is 124 feet long, there had been made holes or mortices,
cut down perpendicularly, 1 foot long, 6 inches broad, and 8 inches
deep. These mortices were directly opposite to each other, and
continued the whole length of the benches, at the distance of $2\frac{1}{2}$
feet from one another. These holes were left when they built
the Gallery, in order to fix into each of them a piece of timber a
foot square, and 3 or 4 feet long ; these timbers and joints made
a scaffold to put the stones on that were necessary to stop up all
the passages that were to be filled up in the inside of the
pyramid, as well as this Gallery, 124 feet in length."

"These joints," he proceeds, "were likewise shaped at the
upper end, so as to be fixed into the mortices of long beams of
wood laid on them, to support planks 6 feet 6 inches long, and
6 inches thick, made very smooth, on which courses of stones
were laid. The benches, as I have said before, being $2\frac{1}{2}$ feet
from the bottom of the Gallery, I suppose the scaffold was set 3
feet above them; so that from the bottom to the scaffold there
was a height of $5\frac{1}{2}$ feet for the workmen to pass backwards and

forwards." He goes on to say, " Perhaps in the body of the pyramid there are other passages stopped up, and not yet dis-covered ; because in the Gallery there might have been placed four or five more courses of stone, if there was occasion."

In another work one may read these words of M. Maillet: " In the benches next the walls there are, at the distance of every 2½ feet, holes 1 foot long, 6 inches broad, and 8 inches deep, cut perpendicularly. The sides of the Gallery rise above these benches 25 feet, twelve of which are exactly perpendicular, at which height it projects 3 inches, and 3 feet higher 3 inches more ; then 3 feet higher it sets out again 3 inches ; and 3 feet higher there is a fourth projection of 3 inches, from which, to the ceiling of the Gallery, which is flat, is 4 feet more ; the ceiling being about the same breadth as the passage between the benches ; that is, about 3 feet 3 inches. This height was necessary to the architect in order *to place the stones intended to fill up the passages*." " Even then," as he adds, " it required 13½ feet of stone to fill up the passage that led to the Royal Chamber, even with the void space at the upper end of the Gallery which they took down from the scaffold to the floor."

But how were the stones brought down from the scaffold ? The ingenious Frenchman has a plan to meet the difficulty, saying : " It is supposed that, in order to facilitate the perform-ance of this work, there was fixed in the floor of the Gallery, over against the stones on the scaffold, a strong machine of iron and substantial pulleys, by the help of which the workmen, standing on the floor, could by ropes take down the stones from the scaffold one after another, and bring them to the very floor."

M. Maillet knew that the great attraction of the whole edifice lay in the King's Chamber, and that near that extra care would be taken to prevent its violation. Whatever treasure lay therein, or whatever were the secrets buried, the design of the builders, strange as it may appear, was for ever, as they expected and hoped, to conceal them from kings and subjects, from priests and laity. He tracks the breakers-in up to this point in the following manner :—

"They found the passage extended further, and was 3 feet 3 inches wide, and well stopped up. It is probable that the last stone was so well fixed as to cost them great labour to remove it; which appears by a piece of the upper stone which was broken off, in order, no doubt, to have a better hold on the lower one, which stopped up the passage. This being removed with great labour, they took out another with the same difficulty; when those two were taken away there appeared a void space 7½ feet long; and, being desirous to clear the way further, they found a third stone, that could not be got out, being every way larger than the hole that it stopped up. This was the last artifice of the architect to deceive any persons that might get so far, and to prevent their looking any more after the private chamber, which is but twelve paces from this place, in which lay the body of the king, and where they would have found the treasure, if any had been deposited with him. Still, this did not discourage the workmen nor deceive them, for they set about breaking the stone, which they must have done with much labour; it was 6 feet long, 4 feet broad, and perhaps 5 or 6 feet high. There was a void space here of 15 feet high, which at the height of 8 feet enlarged itself above 4 feet toward the Gallery, and corresponded to an opening of the passage 18 inches broad, which was 2 feet from the great stone."—"After having cut away the great stone from the place where it was fixed they came at length to the last stone at the entrance of the chamber."

Conscious, as he was, that some might smile at his proposition, he closed thus :—"What I have said in relation to the closing up of the passages of the pyramid and the use of the Gallery will, perhaps, appear new, and bold enough for some critics to call a chimera." There were the stones, most certainly. What was wanted was an explanation of the method of closing; and M. Maillet, in 1692, called his own "a probable system."

The views of Sir H. James, head of the Ordnance Survey, of Sir Edmund Beckett, and of several others, are confirmatory of M. Maillet's conclusions. The portcullis stones were just the size to slide down, as they suppose, on planks to fill the other passages, leaving room for the workmen to pass on the ramps. "The width of the ramps," says one of them, "and, therefore, of the whole Gallery, was wanted for the men to pass by these stones when lying there; and there are besides a series of upright holes in them, evidently for posts, but what the posts were for is not so clear, as the men could easily guide the stones down without them."

Every evidence confirms the idea that the pyramid, on completion, was not intended as a place of visitation or of reference, seeing that it was immediately blocked up.

WHEN WAS THE PYRAMID BUILT?

THIS is not an easy question to solve. We now discover history to be so full of myths that the difficulties of investigation into the past become sensibly increased. The early chronicles of nations are regarded with suspicion. Though we cease to laugh at them, as formerly was done, we are puzzled to interpret what appears on the surface a collection of absurd fables. Egyptian history is not free from false constructions.

Our system of dates did not prevail in olden times. The "year of our Lord" is but some 1200 years old. The Egyptians reckoned events according to the reign of the sovereign. This ancient system is maintained still in England with official documents, as in proclamations and acts of parliament. So long as we keep the list of rulers correctly, time can be fairly estimated. But when, as with Egyptian dynasties, disputes as to authenticity arise, dates are in utter confusion. Elsewhere reference will be made to this philosophical inquiry.

Of course there is one safe mode of reckoning — by astronomical observation. The heliacal rise of the star Sirius, the dog-star, gave the Egyptians the cycle of 1460 years. Any mention of this in the chronicles of a king will give a starting-point in the order of time, though failing to show which cycle of 1460 years is indicated. The year 1322 B.C. was one of these epochs. In 1876 M. Chabas discovered the mention of the heliacal rising of Sirius in the ninth reign of King Menkeres, builder of the third pyramid of Gizeh. Was this 1460 years, or twice that number, before 1322 B.C.? Was he living 2782 B.C., or 4242 B.C.?

No one supposes the Great Pyramid the oldest structure of its kind in Egypt. Sir Edmund Beckett, the German Dr. Lepsius, Mr. H. C. Agnew, and others, are persuaded that the second pyramid is older than the first. While the latter was built by a king of the fourth dynasty, Mr. Birch, of the British Museum, the best English Egyptologist, states that the pyramid of Meydoum was erected by one of the second dynasty. This false pyramid, as it is called, at El-Wasta, is esteemed much older than the Gizeh structures. Tombs of the second dynasty are recognised by Dr. Birch, of the British Museum. The painted statues of the third dynasty were found by Mariette Bey in the Necropolis about the false pyramid of El-Wasta. The present inquiry is limited to the date of the Great Pyramid.

Whatever the age, one thing is clear, that the people were then highly civilised. As Hekekyan Bey remarks, "Had they been merely an agricultural people they could not have disposed of superfluous wealth and labour in prosecuting with such constancy undertakings which were unremunerative." It is equally certain that, as the Rev. Mr. Zincke says, "they had already had a long existence." Some writers thought that, because the Great Pyramid had been raised in the fourth dynasty, only a little time had elapsed since the beginning of the race. The queen's chaplain judiciously observes on this : "Men could not pass in 200 years from the first essays in cutting stone to the grandest stone structure, and in nicety of workmanship one of the most perfect instances of stone joinery that has ever been erected. Some of the pyramids themselves, and many of the tombs, are older than the pyramids of Gizeh. A pyramid has been built in the Faioum as far back as the first dynasty of all." Mr. Kenrick speaks thus of the tombs one sees at the foot of the Great Pyramid : "Their walls are covered with paintings and hieroglyphical inscriptions, which give us as clear an insight into the manners and opinions of the Egyptians under the fourth dynasty as those of Thebes under the eighteenth and nineteenth."

We must be prepared, then, to run back a long way, not only for the date of the pyramid, but for the rise of civilisation in

Egypt. Schliemann's exploration of the site of Troy illustrates the question. He passed through 52 feet of *débris* to the rock, tracing the separate existence of four cities. He shows that the most recent was founded 700 years before our era, and has been destroyed above a thousand years. For historical Troy he claims a date far higher than previously acknowledged. Yet, beneath that he found the remains of a people wholly different from the Homeric Trojans, and yet so long in being that, while the *débris* of the Greek city fills up six feet, the nameless town relics are scattered through nineteen feet of depth.

An attempt to gauge the age of the pyramid has been made by means of the *supposed* chronology of the Bible. But as that has not been settled by theologians themselves, within thousands of years, the laity have little help from clerical labours. Mr. Gliddon tried to make a comparison with the era of the Deluge; but he gave up in utter despair when he ascertained that Jewish and Christian writers gave no less than 300 different dates for that event. Yet many object to Her Majesty's chaplain asserting that the early Scriptures were "to teach to the Israelites religion, and not to teach history to us."

It is not surprising, therefore, that authorities differ about the age of the pyramid. Sayuti, the Arabian historian, was driven beyond the Deluge for its origin, because he could get no reliable information for it this side of the Flood. To show the disagreement, a few dates may be given. While Norden, the old Danish traveller, put it before Memphis was founded, Volney is content to make it 160 years younger than Solomon's temple, or 860 B.C. Because Homer is silent about it, Goguet declares it was raised since the Trojan war. While M. Jomard attributes it to King Venephes, the fourth of the first dynasty, John Greaves, the

Oxford professor, in the time of Charles I., supposes it built about the twentieth dynasty. Kenrick proves that "some of the adjacent tombs contain the shields of kings of the third dynasty.', Sir Gardener Wilkinson writes: "The age of the pyramids themselves is acknowledged by Memphis being already called '*the land of the pyramid*' in the reigns of Suphis, Papi, and Osirtasen, of the fourth, fifth, and twelfth dynasties." M. Renan finds the monuments of Thebes "more modern by 3000 years."

Among precise dates others may be cited; as that of Osburn, 2300 B.C.; Nolan, 2123 to 2171 B.C; Wilkinson, 2200 to 2500 B.C.; Fergusson, 2600 to 3900 B.C; Lesueur, 4000 to 5400 B.C; Bunsen, 3892 B.C. Among those who have further studied history, Dufeu has dates from 4833 to 4923 B.C. Mr. Zincke writes: "We know with equal certainty that they (the pyramids) were built between five and six thousand years ago." Prof. Owen, no mean scientific authority, and no impetuous assertor, assigns "the period of 6109 years from the present date (1875) to the second monarch of the fourth dynasty." Mariette Bey, the founder of the Cairo Museum, and one of the most fortunate of explorers among ruins, puts the fourth dynasty, the era of the pyramids of Gizeh, between 3951 and 4235 B.C. One thing is entirely clear, that the pyramids had ceased to be fashionable at the time of the Hycsos.

In another work, the *Lists of Dynasties* as given by Manetho, the Egyptian historian, will be fully discussed. It is sufficient here to state, amidst the disputations, that the *Lists* are not quite decided. Gliddon is severe, if just, when he says, "Josephus, Eusebius, and Julius Africanus differ so much from each other in the several portions of Manetho's history, of which they present the extracts, that, in their time, either great errors had crept into the then existing copies of Manetho, or one or more of them were corrupted by design; especially in the instance of Eusebius, who evidently suppressed some parts, and mutilated others, to make Manetho, by a pious fraud, conform to his own peculiar and contracted system of cosmogony." Many now can endorse these strictures upon the wily Greek Bishop of Cæsarea, who lived in an age of pious frauds, opposing sects, and mutual persecutions.

M. Rougé, sensible of chronological difficulties, endeavours to lead our minds up to an approximate date, in a review of what took place in Egypt before the Christain era. "If we come to remember," says he, "that the generations which constructed them are separated from our vulgar era, at first, by the eighteen ages of the second Egyptian empire, then by the time of the Asiatic invasion, and afterwards by several numerous and powerful dynasties, which have left us monuments of their passage, the old age of the pyramids, although not able to be calculated exactly, will lose nothing of its majesty in the eyes of the historian."

It is now generally conceded that we have a certain date for the end of the twentieth dynasty; viz. 1300 B.C. Most Egyptologists agree that there are astronomical data for assuming the eighteenth century before Christ as the time of the kings of the eighteenth dynasty. Rougé believes he has full authority for putting the twelfth dynasty at 3000 B.C. It is a long and uncertain clamber thence to Menes of the first dynasty. He was assumed by Josephus, on no recognised data, to live 1300 years before Solomon. Auguste Mariette Bey places him 5000 B.C. Hekekyan Bey says, "The three largest pyramids of Gizeh being geographical monuments, these retrospective measures on the column of Sothic periods were dated to the close of the sixtieth year of the Sothic period ;" this gave 839. M. Dufeu finds the first pyramid date " 789 Nile years after Menes began to reign." Mr. Gladstone, in his *Juventus Mundi*, is satisfied with the high numbers, saying, " Modern Egyptology adopts in general the chronological computations of the priest Manetho, as sufficiently corroborated by the deciphered records of the country."

It is easy to *pooh-pooh* the first eighteen dynasties for which we have to find a place. But we have monuments belonging to kings of most of them, and can read the hieroglyphics they bear. M. Deveria tells his readers that " the first five names of the fourth dynasty are certain." Thus, the era of the Great Pyramid is brought more palpably before us. Without, how-ever, any positive declaration, it may be assumed that English and French Egyptologists are pretty well agreed that the *Great Pyramid was erected about* 6000 *years ago.*

Prof. Piazzi Smyth, of Edinburgh, has, however, come for-ward with certain highly interesting religious speculations respecting the pyramid, which have intensified the popularity of the subject; and, though the great majority of literary and scientific authorities, here and on the continent, are opposed to his theories, he has put forth astronomical arguments for a date of erection which demand thoughtful attention.

He assumes that the Great Pyramid was built 2170 years before Christ. He finds the passage at such an angle, that an observer looking through it 2170 B.C. would observe *the* Polar star (not our present one, but *a* Draconis) below the Pole on the meridian at the equinox. Taking that as a remarkable fact, he *assumes* that the passage was finished at that period. He cites the authority of Sir John Herschel to substantiate his position.

As it is now known that the pyramid was closed absolutely immediately upon completion, Prof. Wackerbarth, of Upsal, takes up his fellow-professor thus :—" This hypothesis is liable to the objection that, the mouth of the passage being walled up, it is not easy to conceive how a star could be observed through it." But this is a fallacious argument; for it may be equally said that, as the coffer or sarcophagus and the King's Chamber were to be for ever shut off from gaze, they had no special meaning in their wonderful measurements. To the question, "What was the use of the passages?" one replies, "The answer is, no use at all, but there they are as a matter of fact; and it is no more improbable that the principal passage was designed with a view to recording its date by the Pole star than that an external shape should have been selected because it satisfied certain mathematical conditions, in themselves of still less use than the recording of a date."

Mr. Smyth has a perfect right to assume a date, and then establish arguments to support it. It was natural that he, as an astronomer, should seek an astronomical origin. But is his discovery of a Polar star then looking down that passage, and in conjunction with the movement of the Pleiades in the opposite side of the Pole on the meridian, any more than a happy coincidence? Because a Draconis was so situated in relation to the passage 2170 B.C., does it necessarily follow that that was the era of construction? Is there anything to prevent Mr. Smyth, or any other man, from selecting another date, earlier or later, which should suit the passing of *another* Polar star on the meridian? Could we not obtain as many ages as we could discover such astronomical coincidences?

As to the weight of Sir John Herschel's authority, it now appears that the worthy man is not responsible for the theory. The Rev. Dr. Nolan naïvely informs us that, "at the request of Colonel Vyse, Sir J. Herschel calculated the place of the star which was Polar at the time when, *according to the reduced chronology*, the pyramids were erected." That is, the date was assumed when an interesting heavenly coincidence fitted it. But against the assumed 2170 B.C. there is the weight of Egyptologists' arguments for a more extended period. As Mr. Smyth is an advocate for supposed Biblical chronology, he must surely find it difficult to account for so vast a progress in government, the arts, and material prosperity, during 178 years, the interval between the Deluge and the erection of the pyramid.

As Noah is stated to have lived 350 years after the Flood, he must have died 172 years after the building of the Great Pyramid, according to the professor and his school of thought. If it be said that men who lived so long added largely to the population, and that, in 180 years, millions could have proceeded from the loins of Noah, it is somewhat remarkable that Holy Scripture shall make Adam 130 at the birth of Seth, Methuselah 187 at the birth of Lamech, and give Noah but three sons in 500 years. Surely the disciples of Mr. Smyth have more reverence for Bible dates than to content themselves with so remote an age as 2170 B.C. While the Hebrew Text gives 352 years from the Deluge to Terah, the Vatican LXX. makes the time 1172 years. They who do not pledge themselves to Usher's chronology, for the Deluge or the Creation, find no difficulty in realising for the era of the Great Pyramid an additional two thousand years.

WHO BUILT THE GREAT PYRAMID?

THE Greeks, who were the talebearers of antiquity, are not always to be relied upon. Not content with telling what they were told, or giving an enlarged version of the same, they too often constructed a pretty story from their own fertile imaginations. The Arabs, as an oriental people, are too fanciful in their narratives. Sober-minded, matter-of-fact Englishmen are quite modern travellers and historians. The question of authorities, therefore, as to the authorship of the pyramid is a puzzling one.

When men looked up at the stupendous building, so dwarfing the structures of their own age, it was quite natural that they should attribute its origin to the giants that lived before the Flood; or, at any rate, to the intellectual giants of that remote period.

An Arab tradition states that Gian ben Gian, the distinguished *pre-Adamite* Monarch of the World, reared it. Firouzabadi was assured that the Adamites very early procured its erection. The Rev. T. Gabb, in 1806, declared it "the production of those immediate descendants of Seth and the Faithful who adhered to them." He meets one supposed difficulty thus :—" Surely," says he, " the immediate descendants of Seth and Enos were of larger stature than we are." In that way he saw how they could lift stones which other men must needs lift " by *jacks*." The very sands at its base made the good man exclaim, "This pyramid must have been erected by the Antediluvians; and the universal Deluge, called Noah's Flood, and the description of it in Holy Writ, will account, in a satisfactory manner, for the lodgment of sands on the surface of the extensive rock." He adds, "These sands, on the subsiding of the waters, were probably very near the summit of the pyramid."

Josephus rehearses the tradition of the Shemites going to Siriad, or Egypt, and erecting there two monuments, one of brick and one of stone, on which they inscribed astronomical discoveries ; and one of these must, it is said, be the pyramid. Mr. John Taylor, the celebrated writer on " The Great Pyramid, Who built it? and Why was it built?" says, " To Noah we must ascribe the original idea, the presiding mind, and the benevolent purpose.   He who built the ark was of all men the most competent to direct the building of the Great Pyramid."

But honest John Greaves, who visited Egypt in 1637, gathering fable and fact in his travels, gives this excellent story from an Arabic book, which he translated :—

" The writer of the book, entitled *Morat Alzeman,* writes: ' *They differ concerning him that built the pyramids. Some say Joseph, some say Nimrod, some Dalukah the queen, and some that the Egyptians built them before the Floud, for they foresaw that it would be, and they carried thither their treasures, but it profited them nothing.   In another place he tels us from the Coptites (or Ægyptians) that these two greater pyramids, and the lesser, which is coloured, are Sepulchers.   In the East pyramid is King Saurid, in the West pyramid his brother Hougib, and in the coloured pyramid Fazfarinoun, the sonne of Hougib.   The Sabæans relate that one of them is the sepulcher of Shiit (that is, Seth), and the second sepulcher of Sab, the sonne of Hermes, from whom they are called Sabæans.   They goe in pilgrimage thither, and sacrifice at them a cocke and a black calfe, and offer up incense.*'

"Ibn Abd Alkokm, another Arabian, discoursing of this Argument, confesses that he could not find amongst the learned men in Ægypt, any certaine relation concerning them. Wherefore *what is more reasonable* (saith he) *then that the pyramids were built before the Floud? For if they had been built after, there would have been some memory of them amongst men;* at last he concludes, *The greatest part of chronologers affirmed that he which built the pyramids was Saurid ibn Salhouk, the King of Egypt, who was before the Floud* 300 *yeares.* And this opinion he confirmes out of the books of the Ægyptians; To which he addes, *The Coptites mention in their books, that upon them is an inscription ingraven; the exposition of it in Arabicke is this:* 'I *Saurid, the king, built the Pyramids in such and such a time, and finished them in six yeares; he that comes after me, and sayes he is equall to me, let him destroy them in six hundred yeares; and yet it is knowne that it is easier to plucke down then to build; and when I had finished them, I covered them with Sattin, and let him cover them with slats.'* The same relation I found in severall others of them."

Josephus, full of the glorification of his people, and having the average oriental disregard of strict veracity, and nearly the average oriental power of constructive invention, inclines to the erection by his forefathers. "The Egyptians," he says, "inhumanly treated the Israelites, and wore them down in various labours, for they ordered them to divert the course of the river (Nile) into many ditches, and to build walls, and raise mounds, by which to confine the inundations of the river; and, moreover, vexed our nation in constructing foolish pyramids." Mr. Yeates suspects they had nothing to do at Gizeh, but may have made brick ones elsewhere. Norden, the Danish traveller, in 1737, has similar doubts, since the Bible spoke of bricks, and not of stone structures there. " As to what concerns the works on which the Israelites were employed in Egypt," he writes, " I admit that I have not been able to find any remains of bricks burnt in the fire." Calmet supposed Moses and Aaron were foremen of the works. Melchizedek is another of the reported builders.

It appears from Herodotus, whose tales are often mystifying enough, that, though Cheops and his brother erected the pyramids, " no Egyptian will mention their names ; but they always attribute their pyramids to one Philition (Philitis), a shepherd, who kept his cattle in those parts." We are further told that this man left Egypt with a following of 240,000 men, and proceeded to the foundation of Jerusalem. Upon this, it is concluded by some that the monuments were erected by the shepherd race. Lord Lindsay says, " There is much reason to believe that they were built by the royal shepherds of Egypt, who afterwards became the Philistines." Mr. Sharpe, the Egyptologist, observes, " The curious remark of Herodotus, that they were called by the name of the shepherd Philitis, is not of sufficient weight against the foregoing reasons to lead us to the conclusion that they were built by the above-mentioned Philistine shepherds." But others have discovered, by arguments convincing to themselves, that this Philitis was none other than the Biblical Melchizedek, seeing that he was King of Salem, that is, of Jerusalem, founded by Philitis.

The shepherd story brings to mind the Hindoo narrative of some early race of India, the Pali, who were a shepherd people, ancestors of the present aboriginal Bheels, succeeding once in conquering Egypt. Their stronghold, *Abaris*, is, in Sanscrit, a *shepherd ; Goshena*, in Sanscrit, is the *land of shepherds*.

We read in the Hindoo Puranas of a war between the gods and the earthborn Yoingees. The latter were vanquished, and retreated to Egypt. Mr. Wilson, the learned writer on the astronomy of the ancients, asks, "Were the Yoingees, the pyramidal builders, instructed in all useful arts, and *spread over all the earth in the earliest ages*, the same as the powerful hierarchy, the pyramidal builders, the constructors of canals for commerce and irrigation, and instructors in the useful arts, that have been traced by their monuments and standards erected in remote ages *round the entire world ?*" The Rev. E. B. Zincke is satisfied that these builders "must have been mainly Aryan ; that is, of the same race as ourselves." Mr. Gliddon, the American Egyptologist, for many years resident on the Nile, writes, "The builders of our pyramids were Mizraimites, children of Ham, of the Caucasian race ;" that is, white men.

Murtadi, the Arab historian, attributes the erection to Bardesi, of Noah's family, who "made the great laws, built the pyramids, and set up for idols the figures of the stars."

Lepsius, the Prussian explorer of the ruins of Egypt, remarks, "It appears that the builders of the Great Pyramids desired to assert their rights to having formed the commencement of monumental history, although it is clear as day that they were *not the first* to build, and to inscribe their monuments." Hekekyan Bey, C. E., defends the memory of those men, who were not mere tyrants. "Despotic governments," he tells us, "seldom, perhaps never, undertake works requiring sacrifice for the benefit of futurity." Yet Aristotle had got the impression that despotic rulers had raised them, and that for the purpose of keeping their subjects poor. Mr. Wilson regards the pyramids as "the monumental rewards" of Sabean missionaries from the East.

Herodotus, the father of history, sometimes appears to know more than he thinks judicious to tell in plain vernacular, and has an esoteric meaning beneath the words. He distinctly gives Cheops the merit of the erection, and the writer found the donkey-boys of Cairo do so still. But M. Chabas is quite wroth at "the ridiculous accounts" of Herodotus; especially at his story of the failure of funds, and the renewal of the same by the self-sacrifice of the king's daughter, who exacted the reward of a stone from each of her lovers.

But who was Cheops, or *Xeopos?* According to one story of the Greek historian, he was an infidel tyrant, who closed the temples of the gods, and was an object of horror to his people. According to the monuments themselves, whose hieroglyphics we are now able to read, he was a pious king, who planned a temple to Hathor, the virgin mother of the gods, offered images of gold and ivory to the gods, and wrote "the Sacred Book." Well may Mr. Birch of the British Museum say, "The religion of the country was already reduced to a system." This Cheops, corrupted by the Greeks to Xeopos, for convenience of sound, was Shoofo. Murtadi, the Arab authority of the sixteenth century, declares that in his day tradition ascribed the building to Soyoof. Memphis is said to have once had a palace called "the abode of Shoopho." Mr. Gliddon alludes to the discovery of the tomb of "Eimei, chief priest of the *habitations* of King Shoopho," near the Great Pyramid; and adds, "This is probably that of the architect, according to whose plans and directions the mighty edifice,—near the foot of which he once reposed,—the largest, best-constructed, most ancient, and most durable of mausolea in the world, was built." We have the name of this king in tablets of the old copper mine of Mount Sinai, whereon he is described as "pure king and sacred priest." The same name occurs on a building in the Thebaid. Eratosthenes speaks of King Saophis, the many-haired; and, in Coptic, *shoo* is *many*, and *pho* is *hair*.

As Khufu or Khoofoo he is also recognised. He is the Suphis of Manetho, the Egyptian historian in the time of the Ptolemies. "Shafra," says Baron Bunsen, "built the upper part of the pyramid, and Khufu the other." Mr. Perring, to whom we are so much indebted for accurate measurements, speaks of two kings —Khufu and his brother Khnemu-Khufu, the latter being the Cheops of Herodotus, though the first erected the Second Pyramid, so called, before the great one was begun. Shafra, or Chephren, further confuses the story. He is styled on the monuments "the Great of the Pyramid," and is called co-regent by Perring. Cheops, Xufu, Souphis, or Suphis, was the successor, though not, apparently, the son, of Snefru, the conqueror of the Sinai peninsula, and whose wife, Mer-t-tefs, allied herself afterwards to Cheops. "A crowd of functionaries of all orders attest to the riches and power of his government," says the *French Archæological Review*.

Mr. Piazzi Smyth whitewashes the character of Cheops from the charges of Herodotus concerning cruelty, impiety, &c. The Professor holds that the Hycsos branch of the Biblical patriarchs were led by Divine influence to invade and subdue Egypt; though, it would appear, only to erect the pyramid, and be off again to Palestine. The quarry marks of the Construction Chambers indicated Cheops and Cephren as the builders. We must, according to his theory, make them Hycsos, and true worshippers of the One God. Here is his defence against the Egyptian calumny :—

" This is what they (the Egyptians) did not forgive ; viz., that
King Shofo (Cheops or Suphis) ' overthrew their temples, and
was the first to put a stop to the sacrifices.'   King Nou-Shofo
(Chephren) afterwards continuing, or at the time assisting in the
same *regime;* and this the Egyptians term ' inflicting on them
every kind of evil.'   Some very good men among the moderns,
without weighing well from whom this testimony comes, and
without considering the reverse teaching of that sacred warning,
' Woe unto you when all men shall speak well of you ! for so
did their fathers to the false prophets,' describe these two
kings as ' given over to every kind of profligacy and wicked-
ness ; ' but had such been their characteristics they could not
have methodised and steadily employed the industry of a
primeval nation through a long period of years so successfully
as to have produced at last, in the Great Pyramid, the largest
and best built monument which the earth has even yet to show."
He then concludes that the hatred of the people " proves that
they, the said two kings, must have been thoroughly Hycsos in
heart, if they were not also in birth and descent."

Pyramid *Facts*, in this instance, as in so many others, present
another story to that of the *Fancies*.   These two kings were
Egyptian.   Hieroglyphics in Egypt, in the pyramid, and at the
peninsula of Sinai, prove them to be ordinary Egyptian kings
of a regular dynasty ; that they were builders, but not destroyers
of temples ; that they adored the heathen deities of the land ;
and that they were altogether un-Hycsos, in the Professor's sense
of that term, in heart as well as birth and descent.

Let us turn aside a moment to get light, if possible, from the
other historian, Diodorus.   This is his story :—" With regard to
the pyramids, there is no agreement either among the native

authorities or the Greek historians. Some say they were built
by Chemmis, Cephren, and Mycerinus. Some assign them to
other names; as the Great Pyramid to Armæus, the second to
Amosis, and the third to Inaros. Some, again, say that the
third pyramid is the tomb of Rhodopis, the courtesan, which was
built by a contribution of several of the monarchs, her former
lovers." Pliny has less to say, declaring that the names of the
builders have been obliterated by time. There is a wonderful
Cinderella tale told about the Rhodopis of Naucratis, whose fairy-
like slipper, being carried off by an eagle, was dropped in the
lap of the king in Memphis, who could not rest satisfied till he
got the owner of the pretty shoe. But we are bothered further
to learn that Nitocris was the fair builder of the Third Pyramid.
As her name, like that of Rhodopis, means *rosy-cheeked*, Lepsius
safely concludes they were both wives of the same Pharaoh.
But an ancient writer has a romantic narrative of a Rhodopis,
who was a fellow-slave to Æsop, and the sister-in-law of Sappho,
the ill-fated poetess; the beauty got decoyed from Greece to
Egypt.

M. Dufeu, a modern and most learned writer upon the
pyramids, regards Snefru as Cephrenus, the last of the third
dynasty of kings, who, upon the completion of the passage of
the Great Pyramid, assumed the name of Soris, the first of the
fourth dynasty, the Saurid of the Arab historians. As this
sovereign was certainly worshipped up to the very time of the
Ptolemies, toward the era of Christianity, Dufeu exclaims,
"Why this deification and this persistent worship if Cephrenus
had not given to Egypt a monument of an importance thus complete for his country?" He is, however, reputed the constructor
of the Second Pyramid, yet he is associated with Khufu in the

quarry marks of the Great Pyramid. A story is told of his daughter being buried in the figure of a cow. We have his statue in diorite in the museum at Cairo. A bas-relief, at Sinai, describes him as " the King of High and Low Egypt, the lord of diadems, lord of truth, hawk of gold, Snefrou," &c. Elsewhere he is called " the great god : " a title given thus early to Egyptian kings. A great authority remarked, " This bas-relief is, at present, the most ancient of the known historical monuments, at least among those which are dated by Cartouches." The tombs of the family of this monarch have been found at Gizeh, near the pyramid.

The discovery, in the very pyramid itself, of quarry marks with the cartouche or oval of the royal builders has settled the question. The hieroglyphics give the name of Shofo. This is the Cheops of Herodotus, the Suphis of Manetho ; which " two names," says M. Chabas, " are the regular transcription of the Egyptian Khoufou." This distinguished French Egyptologist thus refers to the question : "The Great Pyramid of Gizeh has been constructed by King Khoufou, whose legend has been discovered, written *à la sanguine* upon the interior blocks of the chambers of discharge, which the architect has placed upon the ceiling of the great funeral *salle*, to replace the arches. These inscriptions, which have been traced to the moment of construction, decide by themselves alone, in the most incontestable manner, the question of the destination of the pyramid." At the same time, as Chephren is named with him in the pyramid, he was probably a helper in the undertaking.

As some of one particular school of religious thought—Prof. Piazzi Smyth, &c.,—believe Melchisedek, as Philitis, to have been the constructor of the Great Pyramid, others, like Capt.

Tracey, R. N., advance in the theory, and proclaim the very Saviour Himself the builder.

These are the Captain's words in a recent work : " We may from Scripture show that *our Lord, as Melchisedek, had to do with the Great Pyramid, as the Great Architect thereof;* for God, speaking to Job out of the whirlwind, demands of him (Job xxxviii. 18), 'Hast thou perceived the breadth of the earth ? Declare if thou knowest it all.' This implies that none but God Himself could know it, *consequently,* none could have been the architect of the Great Pyramid but one who knew the counsels of the Almighty ; and *who could this be but our Lord Jesus Christ ?* " He further affirms :—" The first appearance of our Lord as Melchisedek, King of Salem, leads me to believe that all His appearances from Babel to Abraham were as Melchisedek." Elsewhere he writes, " Melchisedek was really our Lord."

SMALLER PYRAMIDS OF GIZEH.

THOUGH the Great Pyramid has been the main object of enquiry, some reference to its neighbours will not be out of place.

The plateau of Gizeh, high above the region inundated by the Nile, was selected for a burial-ground in the earliest times of Egyptian history. The pyramids there are but lofty, royal tombs amidst a vast number of sepulchres. But that which excites astonishment is that we should have such noble architectural monuments remaining, appropriated as memorials to deceased princes, priests, and women, with nothing left to mark even the site of towns inhabited by them when living.

The pyramids there are surrounded by graves, not a few of

which are older than the oldest of these pyramids. The Great is called the *First*, because the chief in size and interest. The second is not much its inferior. The third is considerably less, though the most perfect and beautiful. Then come six other structures, of far less extent. Norden, 150 years ago, wrote : "There are four of them that deserve the greatest attention of the curious, though we see seven or eight others in the neighbourhood."

Most of the smaller ones are eastward of the Great Pyramid. Thevenot said, "Before each of the pyramids are the marks of certain buildings, which to some seem to have been so many temples." They were, however, but small pyramids. Doubtless some pyramids have totally disappeared. Before each, as is believed, a temple formerly stood, in which religious rites were performed for the deceased king.

The *Ninth Pyramid* is supposed to have once stood 101 feet in height, though now but 80. The length is 160. It possesses a subterranean chamber $12\frac{1}{4}$ feet long, $9\frac{1}{2}$ wide, and $8\frac{1}{2}$ high.

The *Eighth Pyramid*, to the east of the great one, which it resembles in its work, has been thought the tomb of Cheops' daughter. Its height, once 111, is now 55 feet. The original length was $172\frac{1}{2}$ feet. The funeral chamber is $12\frac{3}{4}$ by $10\frac{1}{4}$ feet.

The *Seventh Pyramid*, according to Mr. F. S. Perring, C. E., had the area of the eighth. It is now but a mound of sand 45 feet high. The chamber is declared $11\frac{3}{4}$ by $9\frac{3}{4}$, with an anteroom, 13 feet 10 inches, by 5 feet 10.

The *Sixth* is south of the third. It had formerly a base of $102\frac{1}{2}$ feet, and height of $69\frac{1}{2}$. There is a passage $47\frac{3}{4}$ feet long, leading to a chamber 26 feet long by 11 feet 4 inches broad.

The *Fifth* is cased with Mokattam marble. It was opened in

1837, when it was described by Col. Vyse and Mr. Perring. The base is 138 feet, but had been 145¾. The height was 93¼, of which 83 feet 4 inches remain; the top is 14 feet. The passage of entry was found 56¾ feet in length, with a horizontal passage, 13 feet 7 inches long, 3 feet 5 inches wide, and 4 feet 1 inch high. The chamber of the dead is 25 feet 6 inches long, 25 feet 2 inches broad, and 8 feet 9 inches high. There was a sarcophagus 6 feet 2 inches long, 1 foot 9½ inches broad, and 2 feet 1 inch deep. Its only contents were some red pottery, burnt reeds, and charcoal. There was no hieroglyphical writing.

The *Fourth Pyramid* is of deeper interest, though small in size. Herodotus referred to it. It is the middle one of the southern group. Norden charges Greaves with applying to the third what should have been said of the fourth. "Its summit," says the Dane, "is of a yellow stone, of the quality of that of Portland." The top is called a *cube*. The height is put at 69½ feet, but was once 82. The base is called 153 by Bunsen, though Perring found it 102½. An inclined passage, at the angle of 27°, is 27 feet long, 3½ wide, and 3¼ high. It leads to a chamber 19 feet 2 inches long, 8 feet 9 wide, and 10 feet 4 high. The granite sarcophagus was 5 feet 10 inches long, 1 foot 6 wide, and 1 foot 11½ deep. There were no hieroglyphics about it; and the contents were bones, earth, and wood-ashes. According to Chevalier Bunsen, it was the tomb of Mycerinus II. The Fourth and Sixth Pyramids differ from the rest in being Pyramids of Degrees, not of ordinary steps.

THE THIRD PYRAMID. Bélon, in 1548, said, "it is yet entire, having no touch of ruin." Villamont saw it in 1589, and reported that it was "built entirely of marble." As the lower half of the casing is of granite, and the upper of marble, the French traveller failed in his observation, or was in fault with mineralogy. He mentioned that it was "entirely preserved." That it was well covered appears from his surprise that no steps were left to mount by. But a determined effort was made toward the end of the eighteenth century to break into it, and a number of stones were withdrawn. The height of the granite is 36 feet 9 inches on the western side, and 25 feet 10 inches on the northern.

This is usually called the Pyramid of Mycerinus, or Menkeres, and was built not very long after the first. Some say that the rosy-cheeked Nitocris was buried there. The granite casing has given it the appellation of the Red Pyramid. The twelve lower courses of the casing are of red granite. Much was removed before Mehemet Ali carried off the fine slabs. After the failure of others, Col. Vyse succeeded in effecting an entrance on the north, in 1837. Though a passage partly lined with granite ran 104 feet, at an angle of 26° 2′, all other parts were solid, and the chambers had to be hewn out of the mass. The Mamelukes had attempted a breaking in at 71 feet from the base. The lower excavation is 35 feet from the base.

The entrance was most carefully hidden. The passages and the chambers were closed by the fall of the portcullis, or filled with blocks of stone, the same as with the Great Pyramid. The base is 354½ feet. The height, now but 203, was formerly 261. The square top is about 16 feet; the angle of the side is 51°. The anteroom—at the bottom of the incline—found filled with stones—is 12 feet long, 10 feet 5 inches wide, and 7 feet high. There is a large room with the dimensions of 46 feet 3 inches by 12 feet 7 inches, and from 12 feet 11 inches to 13 feet

4 inches in height. The Sepulchral Chamber beneath the east end of the large apartment is 21 feet 8 inches long, 8 feet 7 wide, 11 feet 3 inches high. The pentroof was of two huge blocks of stone. The chamber was lined with $2\frac{1}{2}$ feet thick granite slabs, fastened by iron cramps. The passages were lofty, being 4 feet 9 inches high.

The sarcophagus was the great object of interest. Mr. Vyse, before reaching this spot, guessed from appearances that some one had been before him. The ramps had been inserted after the coffer had been placed. The outside measurement of the basaltic tomb was 8 feet long, 3 feet 1 inch wide, 2 feet 11 high; the inside, 6 feet 5 inches, by 2 feet $0\frac{1}{2}$ inches, and 2 feet $0\frac{1}{2}$ inches deep. If a passage had been forced, the body had been removed before the enclosure. Bunsen thinks it was removed by the ancient Egyptians. There is a tradition mentioned by Edrisi, 1245, of a corpse having been seen there, and that beside it were golden tablets inscribed with unknown characters.

The interesting, but *lidless*, sarcophagus, weighing three tons, was despatched to London in 1838. Unfortunately the vessel sank with its burden near Gibraltar. The Mummy Board, however, came safely to the British Museum. On this is a prayer to Osiris. Though the tomb was partially opened by Count Caviglia, it was first explored by Col. Vyse in 1837.

THE SECOND PYRAMID. Upon the observation of Herodotus that this was 40 feet lower than the Great Pyramid, Mr. Agnew writes, "He could neither mean the perpendiculars of the pyramid nor the line bisecting the face." It needs interpretation, like the Arab tradition, that there once stood upon the top an image of gold 40 cubits high.

According to Arabian authority, the coating was entire at the beginning of the twelfth century. Mr. Agnew remarks that "the darkish colour which the surface has acquired seems to have led some travellers into the error of supposing that the Second Pyramid was cased with granite." Bélon, in the sixteenth century, speaks of it being cemented outside; and adds that "the part which looks to the north is consumed with humidity." Thevenot wrote, "The Second Pyramid is shut up, and has no steps without." Though covered in 1638, the marble now comes but from 130 to 150 feet from the top. The lower tiers, says Herodotus, were faced with granite. The casing is 130 feet on one side, and 150 on the other. The top, broken somewhat, is 8 feet in extent.

A curious report is believed by some, that a Cufic inscription has been seen upon the top. It has not been copied, and the toeing of the crevices in the marble casing is not safe for even the agile Arab, who will now, for a franc, run from your side on the platform of the Great Pyramid down to the sands, and up to the casing of the second, in a marvellously short time. There is a pavement below, some 36 feet broad. The building contains 65,928,000 cubic feet, with a weight of 4,883,000 tons.

The base, once 707¾ feet, is now 690¾, according to Perring; 684, by Belzoni; and 695, by Wilkinson. The height, says Sir Gardner, was 466, and is 439 feet; but, by Perring's measure, 454¼ once, and 447½ now. Belzoni made 456 feet above the pavement; which, deducting 15 for the pedestal, leaves 441. Three feet have been lost from the top. It stands upon 11 acres, or two less than its neighbour. The rock was levelled for its construction. Mr. Agnew noticed that "the diagonals of the two Great Pyramids which join the south-west and north-east corners are in the same direction, but not quite in the same line." The angle is placed by him at 52° 25′ 17″. The second has nearly the same orientation as the first, from which it is only 500 feet removed.

This pyramid is generally attributed to Khenun Khufu, or Shafra, brother of Cheops, the builder of the first pyramid. By the Greeks the builder is named Chephrenes, Chephren, or Cephren. His statue, cut out of diorite, and found in the pit of the Sphinx temple, is a magnificent piece of art, and exhibits quite a Caucasian style of face. Mr. Agnew considers that the second was commenced before the first was finished, and the third was begun before the completion of the second. The proportion of the second to the first is as 7 is to 8.

Belzoni, in 1818, had the good fortune to open this pyramid. The Arabs usually call it after him now. He found the portcullis difficulty in the passages. Chambers are made in the solid masonry; some are above the base, and others in the rock. Two entrances lead to the interior; the upper, 50 feet from the base; the lower, beneath the pavement. The Upper Passage has an angle of 26° 41′, according to Bunsen; but Perring makes it 25° 55′. It is 3 feet 5½ inches wide, and 5 feet 10 inches high. The length to Belzoni's chamber is 128 feet 4 inches; but 104 feet 10 inches to the Horizontal Passage. The latter is 27 feet long, 5¾ wide, and 3 high. Both passages are lined with granite. The lower inclined passage is 96—4 × 3—5½ × 3—11 high. The angle is 22° 15′. It is 100 feet from the portcullis to the mouth of the lower entrance. The portcullis was 15 inches thick. It guarded the passage to the sepulchral chamber. Excepting a portion of the upper passage, all the excavations are below the level of the base.

The chamber called Belzoni's, having a painted roof, is 46 feet long, 16 wide, and 22½ high.   There is another 11 × 6 feet.   The lower sepulchral chamber, whose roof is 90 feet below the base of the pyramid, is said by Perring to be 34 feet 1 inch long, 10 feet 2 inches wide, and 6 feet to 8 feet 5 inches high.   The sar-cophagus, found buried level with the floor, measured on the outside 8 feet 7 inches by 3 feet 6½ inches, and 3 feet high; on the inside, 7 feet by 2 feet 2½ inches, and a depth of 2 feet 5 inches.   It was of granite, and had no hieroglyphics.

No body was discovered, though bones of the Sacred Bull were lying near.   Diodorus heard that the priests, who cordially hated the monarch, forbade his corpse being conveyed thither. As the floor exhibited marks of disturbance, Mr. Perring dug down 36 feet; but without finding anything.

Some hieroglyphics have been discovered near the north-west angle.   A tradition exists that one Mohammed Ahmed opened the pyramid a thousand years ago.   Chevalier Bunsen says, " This pyramid, as well as those of earlier date, to which it as-similates in every respect, has no chambers in the inside, but that it merely covered with its artificial giant top the sepulchral chamber hewn out of the rock under its centre."   Several writers imagine from the rudeness of its structure, and inferiority of its workmanship, that it preceded the Great Pyramid by many years.

OTHER EGYPTIAN PYRAMIDS.

MEMPHIS was situated ten miles south of the Great Pyramid. Once the capital of Egypt, about ten miles from the apex of the Delta, and still called *Memf* by the Copts, it must have been an immense city, flourishing an enormous period.   Abd'allatif, 600 years ago, described its ruins as covering a great space. Bakoui, of the fifteenth century, was wonderstruck at them. Furer, in 1565, spoke of two gigantic statues there, 20 feet high, with many stone animals. Radziwil, 1583, mentions a figure 20 cubits long lying on the ground. Abulfedu was delighted with the freshness of the colours. But Memphis has now scarcely a ruin to be recognised.

The Necropolis of *Saqqarah*, whose tombs extend four or five miles, was the City of the Dead for Memphis. In the midst of these sepulchres rose some pyramids. In Pococke's Travels, 1743, eleven of them are marked down. Jomard gives sketches of some, and marks the differences among them. Denon, 1799, talks of there being thirty; and adds, " one finds traces of a great number of others." Inside the truncated one to the south were found chambers with niches, as in the Third Pyramid of Gizeh.

The age of Saqqarah is greater than that of Gizeh. We read that Ouenephes, fifth king of the first dynasty, built pyramids at Cochome, supposed to be Saqqarah. The Serapeum, or burial-place of the sacred Apis bulls, is at Saqqarah, and was discovered in 1861.

The Great Pyramid of Saqqarah, or Pyramid of Degrees, though allowed to be " exceptional " by Mr. Fergusson, is fancied by him " an imitation of the old form of mausolea by some king of a far more modern date." But his doubtful mind is seen in another place, where he writes that it is " of a date *either an-terior or posterior* to these " (other pyramids). Though an architect, he does not profess to be an Egyptologist. But Dr. Birch, a real authority, says clearly that " it is the oldest Egyptian monument hitherto found." Mariette Bey is positive that it belongs to the first dynasty. He attributes it to the fourth king of the first dynasty.

It has six steps, or degrees. The material is stone and rubble. In size it corresponds with the Third Pyramid of Gizeh. From north to south it is 351 feet; east to west, 394. The height is $200\frac{1}{2}$ feet. The angle of the face is 72° 36'. Each story is said to be " not built in horizontal courses, but a pyramidal nucleus of rubble is inclosed by a series of inclined walls, about 9 feet thick, eleven in number on each side of the central mass, with an additional one on the north and south sides. These walls are composed of rudely-squared stones, set to the angle of the face."

Baron Minutoli, of Genoa, had the honour of revealing the interior, in 1824. Of his interesting collection, the greater part was lost in shipwreck; a few things were purchased for the Berlin Museum. His wife has left us some interesting details of his work. Among these is the account of the many passages, corridors, and chambers, " in the walls of which," says she, " were encrusted convex pieces of porcelain, of various colours, which, when seen by torch-light, must have a pretty effect. There are also *hieroglyphics above several doors,* a circumstance which has not hitherto been remarked in the other pyramids. The largest of these chambers, the walls of which were blackened by the smoke of the torches, contained, instead of a sarcophagus, a small sanctuary, formed of several blocks of stones." The vitrified bluish-green porcelain slabs lining the chamber are like Dutch tiles.

Mr. Vyse found the horizontal passage below level, and a pit leading to the Subterranean Chamber. This passage is 120 feet long, and conducts to the pit. There are, however, four en-

trances. The main passage is 176 feet long. The Great Chamber, 77 feet in height, is in the centre of the pyramid, and is 24
feet by 23 in size. This sepulchral chamber contained no sarcophagus. One writes thus of it:—"Immediately under the
centre of the pyramid there is an excavation 77 feet in depth,
24 by 23 in width, entirely in the rock. Its upper part was
originally covered by a ceiling of wood."

In the granite floor was seen a small chamber 10 feet by $5\frac{1}{4}$,
with its entrance closed by a huge granite stone, weighing four
or five tons. This may have been a treasury, or was once used as
an oracle, says somebody. There are two smaller rooms, one
being $20\frac{1}{2} \times 5 \times 6\frac{1}{2}$ feet ; and the other, $18\frac{1}{2} \times 5 \times 6\frac{1}{2}$ feet. Baron
Minutoli found a skull gilded over, and two gilt soles of feet.

The most northern pyramid of Egypt is Abouroash, five miles
north-west of Gizeh. But it is properly described as "very
much degraded, and contains nothing of importance." There
is also a very-much-ruined pyramid a little south of Gizeh.

In general, the Egyptian pyramids may be said to be in a
line from the north-east. There are, says Mr. Casey, thirty-eight
pyramids on the western side of the Nile, between lat. 29° 59′
and 29° 26′ ; or, in about thirty miles. There are twenty-five in
a line of twenty-five miles.

A couple of miles north of the Saqqarah ten pyramids, and
seven or eight miles south-east of Gizeh, are the pyramids of
ABOUSIR. Herodotus tells us that an inscription upon the
celebrated brick pyramid said, "Do not disparage me by comparing me with the stone pyramids. I am as superior to them
as Amoun is to the gods." The bricks are of excellent quality,
16 inches long, 8 broad, and 5 thick.

The North Pyramid of Abousir, called Sahuras, is 257 feet long, and 163 high, bearing the angle of 51° 42′ 35″. Its chamber is 11½ feet long, and 12½ high. It is built on the sand. The Great Pyramid of Abousir was 359¾ feet long, and 228 high; but is now 325 long, and 164 high. The passage leading to the Sepulchral Chamber is 104 feet in length. Wood has been found there quite sound, though brittle. In the British Museum is the branch of a tree taken out of the masonry. One, described as 80 feet above the soil, had formerly an elevation of 215. The fourth and fifth pyramids appear not to have been finished.

The Central Pyramid of Abousir had once a base of 274 feet, and a height of 171; it stretches now 213 feet long, and is 107 high. The passage was ascertained to be 63 feet long, 5 wide, and 6 high. The fourth monarch of the fifth dynasty is said to have been buried in the Middle Pyramid, and the fifth king in another. The seventh was interred in the neighbourhood. Both the second and third of the fifth dynasty are also supposed to have been buried at Abousir. Snefru-nub-Ra found his last home there.

DASHOOR, in the neighbourhood of Saqqarah, Abousir, and Memphis, boasts of five pyramids. They are much dilapidated. The north brick one is said to have been built by King Sasychis, the early legislator, the eleventh of the Memphite sovereigns. One, half the height of the Gizeh Pyramid, has a slope of 54°, but is finished off at the angle of 45°. While the North one shows a length of 326½ feet, it formerly had 342½. The South is of stone, with a base of 320 feet. The Large Pyramid has 198 steps. There are 68 forming a height of 184 feet, at the angle 54°; and 130 smaller stones in a height of 250 feet, at 45°. The base is 600 feet.

The Pyramid of Lisht is nine miles south of Dashoor.

MEYDOUN Pyramid, twelve miles south of Lisht, is half way from Cairo to Beni-souef. In its Necropolis were discovered the much-admired statues of Ra-hotep and his wife Nefer-t, of the time of Snefrou, last of the third dynasty. Meydoun Pyramid was, doubtless, the tomb of Snefrou, the predecessor of Khufu or Cheops. But Dr. Birch gives it even higher antiquity, assigning it to Nefer-Ra-ra, the last but one of the second dynasty!

Meydoun has more the appearance of a tower than a pyramid. Its slanting walls, of several terraces, have gained for it by the Arabs the name of the *False* or *Lying* Pyramid. It is a diminishing cube, with a similar cube on the top. Though situated on a low plain, it is out of the reach of inundations. The angle is 74°. For 120 feet upward, nothing but rubbish is seen. But 100 feet higher a platform is gained. A third elevation follows. Some one writes, "Two smaller towers rise from its summit, in the manner in which it is supposed Assyrian pyramids were usually constructed."

It has been conjectured that there were successive stages, 40 feet each, while the steps were filled up afterwards. Some think it has never been completed, though begun in degrees. In the Necropolis of Meydoun, Mariette Bey found the painted statues of the third dynasty, described as the "oldest specimens of Egyptian art." Dr. Birch refers the Meydoun statues of El Wasta Necropolis to the age of the third dynasty.

Incidentally we drop upon quite a number of the *names* of pyramids upon the ancient monuments. On steles we read of those of Asse-nefer, of Ra-tet-ke'-nefer, of Pepi of the sixth dynasty, of Meri-en-ra of the sixth, of Ra-nefer-re men-ankh of the sixth, of Ra-tep-ke-nefer, of Man-nefer, of Pepi-men-nefer, of Ra-meri-en scha-nefer of the sixth dynasty, of Amenu of the eleventh dynasty, &c.   But where are these pyramids?

In the *Fayoum*, says Mr. Zincke, are some " as far back as the first dynasty of all."   Denon speaks of one there, Hilahoun, —" The most ruinous of all the pyramids I have seen, is also that built with the least magnificence.   Its construction is composed of masses of calcareous stones, which serve as a nest for a heap of unbaked brick."   In the Fayoum are ruins of very massive masonry, with the remains of a pyramid at the south-east corner, having a slope of 67°.

This is the neighbourhood of Lake Mœris, the artificial basin of water, formerly, as one has reported, 30 miles, and another 190 miles, round.   Herodotus says there were two large pyramids rising out of the lake, above 500 feet in height.   He says the height above the surface equalled that beneath it.   The total, 100 orgyes, or a stadium, was 600 Babylonian feet.   Mœris is said—so reports John Greaves—to have erected " one for himself, and the other for his wife, placing upon them two marble statues, sitting on a throne, imagining by these works he should propagate to posterity an immortal memory of his worth."   Elsewhere we learn that the two were erected for Amenemha III., and his sister.

The *Labyrinth* was near these.   It contained 3600 rooms in two stories.   Lepsius, who explored its ruins, writes, " We have obtained an entry into a chamber covered with piles of rubbish that lay before the pyramid, and here we also found the name of Amenemha several times.   The builder and possessor of the pyramid is   therefore determined."   This Pyramid of the Labyrinth was 240 feet high.   It rose from the rock, and was

of brick cased with stone. Examination proves that the bricks
—17½ inches long by 8¾ wide, and 5½ thick—had not been
baked; much straw was laid in fine gravel to form them. The
Amenemha was a king of the twelfth dynasty.

Alongside the Labyrinth was the Pyramid of Osymanduas,
raised, as Diodorus relates, at the expense of twelve kings, and
having a girth of gold measuring 360 cubits. The astronomical
character of this will be apparent. Dr. Lepsius found three in
the place of one pyramid at Abu Roash, and ascertained that two
had stood near Zaniet el Arrian.

Greaves, who rambled to the Fayoum 240 years since, refers
thus to more pyramids :—"There are others in the Libyan
Desert, where it bounds Egypt, of which there is no particular
mention extant, either in the Greeks, Latines, or Arabians,
unlesse we shall apply these words of Diodorus to some of
them : 'There are three other pyramids, each side of which
conteine two hundred feet, the structure of them, excepting the
magnitude to the former (at Gizeh). These three kings before
mentioned (Chemmis, Cephren, and Mycerinus) are reported to
have erected them for their wives.' But if these three kings,"
continues Mr. Greaves, "built them for their Queenes, it may
be wondred why they should have placed them so remote from
their owne Sepulchers, or why they should stand at such large
and inequall differences of severall miles from one another."

The *Ethiopian* or *Nubian* pyramids have given rise to much
controversy. Some declare they are the most ancient of all,
while others recognise no such antiquity.

Mr. Hoskins speaks of the eighty pyramids of Meroe, the old
capital of Ethiopia, near the junction of the White Nile with the
Blue, though it stood on the former stream. Noting their isola-

tion, he says the pyramids are " not surrounded by any architectural ruins of the city itself, and which are actually fifty miles
from the remains of a single temple." He counted thirty-five near
Nouri, with no appearance of ruins near, and seventeen at Gibel
el Birkel, where there is a portion of an old temple, and whose
sepulchres he deemed the " most modern in Ethiopia."

While he regards them as older than those of Lower Egypt,
Mr. Gliddon calls them more recent. For all that, the American
traveller admits that they were " all ancient in the days of Tirhaka, 700 B.C." Allowing an average of twenty-two and a half
years for the life of a king, and every pyramid to represent a
royal tomb, he gets for the 139 Nubian pyramids the building
term of $3027\frac{1}{2}$ years.

Dr. Lepsius affirms that of 139 Nubian monuments, all of
sandstone, eighty are at Meroe, having a base of from 20 to 60
feet; forty-two are at Nouri, with a length of from 20 to 100;
and seventeen at el Birkel, 23 to 80 feet in extent. They are of
different sorts, arched, pointed, and round. He thinks them
rather modern. He discovered the remains of sixty-seven
pyramids altogether. Mr. Waddington is of Mr. Hoskins'
opinion, remarking that " the utter destitution and shapelessness
of many of the pyramids of Nouri and el Birkel attest their
antiquity." One has an arched roof of five stones, with a key-
stone. Its base is 159 feet, and height 103.

One, having the remarkable angle of 70°, was opened by Dr.
Guiseppo Ferlini of Bologna. Many resemble the Mexican
mounds. Some have porches, and pointed, Gothic-like arches.
Most are small, but tall for their size. The author of *Egypt and
Mehemet Ali* has an interesting notice of these Nubian monuments, from which a few extracts may be here given :—

"Two groups of pyramids stand near Djebel-Birkel, in Nubia ; one contains only a few pyramids. None of these pyramids are above 80 feet high, and they are comparatively smaller at the base than the Egyptian pyramids, and more tapering. Only a few of these pyramids had sculptures, which were softer and more voluptuous than the Egyptian style admits. I think the majority of the pyramids of Noar to be the most ancient of all the Ethiopian monuments now extant. They are not so taper as the pyramids of Birkel, and consequently more nearly resembling the Egyptian. The remains of more than forty may be distinguished, but only sixteen of them are in tolerable preservation." Of one it is said, "The form of this singular structure differs entirely from those which surround it ; and it appears to have consisted of several stories, of various degrees of steepness. The entire height of this truncated pyramid, as it now stands, is nearly 100 feet, and its circumference about four times that extent."

If the Nubian were the older, the conclusion would be that civilisation and the pyramid-building art descended the Nile ; but the strength of opinion inclines to the belief that Nubia was a colony of Egypt, and civilised by the men of Thebes and Memphis.

OTHER MONUMENTAL TOMBS.

THE *Mexican Pyramids*, or *Teocallis*, were erected, according to the theory of some, by a particular masonic body, known as *pyramid builders*, the remains of whose labours are to be seen from China, by India, Persia, Egypt, Barbary, and across America, to the South Sea Isles.

There is a plain in Mexico called Micoatl, the *Path of the*

Dead, where hundreds of teocallis are seen, and which served as burying-places. They are truncated pyramids. Their tops served as altars, and human victims were often hurled down the steps of the edifice. Not unfrequently a temple or priest's building stood at the top.

Like as in the pyramids of Egypt, the sepulchral chamber was subterranean, and was usually entered from the exterior by a short vertical descent, and a long horizontal passage. They were, therefore, both tombs and temples. At times they served as forts, or as royal palaces. They existed long before the arrival of the Aztecs, with whom the Spaniards came in contact. Their ornamentation has been despoiled by the conquerors.

The Teocalli of Cholula, upon a plain 6000 feet high, has a base twice the size of the Great Pyramid of Egypt. It is 1589 feet long, and is 180 high, being built of unburnt bricks. An image to a god formerly stood on the summit. The pyramids of Teotihuacan, on the plain of Otumba, are twenty-five miles northeast of the city of Mexico. There are hundreds of small ones round a larger. The central part is made of clay and small stones, and the outer wall is of basaltic stone. On one was formerly an image of the sun, covered with plates of gold, which were stripped off by Cortez. This edifice was 682 feet base, and 180 high. The Pyramid of the Moon, near it, was 36 feet shorter. The Pyramid of Papantla, near the Gulf of Mexico, has six or seven stories. Three staircases lead outside to the top. Yucatan has several pyramids, which are very ancient. Oaxaca has a symbolical spiral tower of nine stages.

PERU has its pyramids. That of Pachacamac has a base of 500 by 400 feet, with a height of 250. Brick pilasters project from the uppermost wall. The temple of Tiaguanico is a stone-terraced pyramid.

The MOUND BUILDERS of Ohio, &c., were of long past ages. Their vast edifices are the only memorials of their existence. One near the Mississippi is 420 feet long, and 390 broad at the base, while the top is 120 by 100.

INDIA has pyramids in the Peaks of Menu. The pyramidal entrances of pagodas resemble the propylæa of temples in Egypt. The pagoda of Tanjore rises 200 feet; and the shrine of Juggernaut 350. Near Ellora, so famous for its sculptured caves, there are three pyramidal edifices without sculptures. North Ceylon possesses some in the form of truncated pyramids. Java has a seven-terraced pyramid on a mound. It is called Bora Bodu temple, and is 620 feet at the base, and 100 high. The Javanese temple of Suku has three stories.

NINEVEH and BABYLON had their pyramids. The Tower of Babel, or the Tower of Nimrod, is thus described by Mark Gregory, who saw it in 1712. "'Tis a tower exactly square; that is, having four sides, equal, in form of an obelisk or pyramid." It had nine flat cubes. Raised then 162 feet, it seemed to lack a third of its height. He says, "It wanted the ninth story for its completion, and terminated with a round flat of 54 feet diameter, having an aperture or hole of 9 feet, being the window of the temple, as above, in the middle; and it continues so to this day." Alas! since his day it has undergone strange changes.

Herodotus describes it as "four square, and each side being two furlongs in length. In the midst of this holy place there is a solid tower of the thickness and height of a furlong." Dr. Smith's History states that "the axis of the building, or line joining the centres of the stages, was inclined to the horizon; and if we imagine the building enclosed by lines joining the corresponding corners of the steps, the figure so formed would be an oblique pyramid." M. Ernest Pillon says that six of the eight stories have gone, and that the two left can be seen at a distance of six miles. The base he calls 194 metres, or about 640 feet. The bricks were of pure white clay, stamped with characters before burning; bitumen was also used.

The Mujelibe, once supposed the Tower of Belus, was found by Mr. Rich of brick, 200 yards on the north, 219 south, 182 east, and 136 west. The highest part left was 141 feet. Its circumference, 2111 feet, was nearly that of Babel or Birs Nimroud, 2286. He reckoned the latter 235 feet in height, and the side of the square, 571½ feet.

CHINA, in its pagodas and its nine-storied temples, has pyramidal structures. Some have been found in Tartary, and even Southern Siberia.

The PACIFIC ISLANDS bear the same impress of pyramid builders, who worked there when the area of land was far more extensive than at present. Ancient stone buildings of this shape appear in Hawaii, and other islands of the North Pacific. The Pyramid of Atehuru, in Polynesia, is of stone, 270 feet long, 94 wide, 50 high, with a flat top. The *Morai*, or temple of Maeva, is 120 feet square; and that of Oberea is 267 long, 87 broad, and 44 high. On Easter Island, now isolated and uninhabited, in the South Pacific, where enormous images of stone testify to a very advanced civilisation, and, therefore, much greater expanse of land, there is seen an immense mound of earth 384 by 324 feet, with a platform of cut stone 80 feet long, 12 broad, 8 thick.

The following account of the curious pyramids on the tomb of the Etruscan king, Porsenna, is by Varro: "He was buried outside Clusium city, in which place he left a monument of square stone. Each side of it was 300 feet broad, and 50 high. Upon this square there stood five pyramids, four in the corners and one in the middle. In the base they were 75 feet broad, and 150 high. They were pointed in such a manner that at the top there is a brass circle and covering for them all, from which there hang bells, fastened to chains. These being moved by the wind give a sound afar off, as at Dodona it has formerly been. Upon this circle there are four other pyramids, each of them 100 feet high; above which, on a plain, there are five pyramids." There were, therefore, three tiers of pyramids.

Only mere fragments remain to illustrate the civilisation of the past. But for a few monuments we should perceive no relics of races long passed from the earth. Because Egypt has material to show the existence of a high development of progress in the arts some seven thousand years ago, it is not to be assumed that all other lands were then in darkness.

OBELISKS.

THE removal of the so-called Cleopatra's Needle to our own shores gives the obelisk a new interest. Geometrically allied to the pyramid, it is fitting that a reference be made to it here. The mathematical, scientific, and symbolical account cannot be discussed on the present occasion.

The avenues of obelisks leading to the temples of the Middle and New Empires, and the frequency of their use as memorial stones, would, at first, seem to imply their sole employment in those epochs. The researches of Egyptologists have brought out the fact that they were not uncommon under the Ancient Empire itself. While the one standing at Heliopolis is proved to belong to the very remote twelfth dynasty, or nearly 5000 years, others were far older; as Mr. John Wilson says : "This form of a monument, which plays so conspicuous a part in the New Empire, is thus thrown back some dynasties further into the Old Empire than even the obelisk at Heliopolis." Dr. Lepsius found one in a cemetery of the seventh dynasty at Gizeh. Each pyramid appears to have formerly had an obelisk in front, as a sort of satellite.

Easily thrown down and destroyed by political or religious fanatics, and, from being so graceful an ornament, easily removed to the distant home of conquerors or *dilettanti*, it is not surprising that but seven are found now standing in Egypt; viz., four at Thebes, one at Philæ, one at Alexandria, and one at Heliopolis. England has four, France has two, Florence has two, Constantinople has two, but Rome has twelve. Twelve were recently counted lying down in the Nile valley. It is said that, as no pyramids have been found on the east side of the Nile, so no obelisks are to be beheld on the other bank. It is, moreover, singular that the proportions of Nebuchadnezzar's image,—probably a gilded obelisk,—namely, 60 to 6, should have characterised at least some of the obelisks. Thus, there was said to have been one 60 cubits high, and 6 broad, as in Babylon. Pococke saw one near Medinet-el-Faioum, that was 43 feet high, and 4 feet 2 inches broad on the northern face.

Herodotus mentions a fine obelisk 100 cubits high. Reckoning a Babylonian cubit at 8·43 inches, this may have been the Citoria, so admired by tourists in Rome, which was brought by Augustus, and is 71 feet 5 inches. That raised by Sesostris,

120 cubits, will correspond to the tall monument before St. Peter's Church, 83 feet 2 inches; and nearly to that now in Paris, 81 feet. The magnificent one at the Lateran is 150 cubits, or 105 feet 7 inches. The Flaminian, introduced by Augustus, is 73 feet. The one at St. Peter's, strictly speaking, is 77·18 feet in the shaft, 8·83 in the base, and 5·91 in the pyramidal top. These parts in the Lateran one are respectively, 97·5, 9·716, and 6·77; and in the Flaminian, of the Piazza del Popolo, 73 feet, 7·83, and 4·83.

Cleopatra's Needle has a shaft of only $57\frac{1}{2}$ feet. Just before last Christmas, when the writer saw it, this fine relic of the past was in a most disgusting and noisome condition. In 1801, our soldiers and seamen in Egypt, having vanquished the French there, were delighted with the proposal to carry off the Alexandrian obelisk as a trophy, and gave up a day's pay to meet the expected charges. But the General arrested the movement. In 1819, Mehemet Ali made a present of it to our Prince Regent; the calculated cost of removal delayed the sending for it. The *White Elephant* was subsequently offered to, and declined by, the Crystal Palace managers. Cleopatra did not order the construction of the obelisk called after her name; she merely brought it from Heliopolis, where it had adorned the Temple of the Sun, and placed it, as a compliment to the Roman, in the Cæsarem of Alexandria.

Although more or less associated with idolatrous emblems, it may not be held necessary to perform for our London visitor a ceremony deemed essential for a fellow-obelisk removed to Rome. This one was solemnly exorcised by Pope Sixtus V., that no malignant god of Egypt retain supernatural hold upon the stone, or blight the Christian beholder.

The appellation of *Needle* is an old one, and very appropriate. We have Abenesi's remarks on these edifices : "The priests of Egypt erected these elevated stones in the form of needles, and of a round figure ; they engraved there, in mystical characters, the secrets of their philosophy, and called them the altars of their gods."

The one at Heliopolis is, like almost all others, of red granite, from the quarries of Syene, on the Nile. The town of Heliopolis, so celebrated for its ancient Temple of the Sun, in which, most probably, the father-in-law of Joseph officiated as high-priest of the god, was in ruins even in Strabo's day. Herodotus speaks of two fine obelisks there. Abd-al-Latif saw there two, though one had fallen and was broken in two parts ; he calls them, in his Arabic narrative, *Pharaoh's needles.* Pococke made the solitary stranger in the waste $67\frac{1}{2}$ feet high, 6 feet on the north and south base, and 6 feet 4 inches on the east and west. An Arab traveller, in 1190, saw a pyramid of copper on the summit; that is now wanting.

It is traced by Mariette Bey, as far back as to Ammanemes II., 3300 B.C., or over 5000 years ago. Others had attributed it to Osirtasen, of the twelfth dynasty, near the same epoch. This was above 1000 years before the visit of Abraham to Egypt, and long before the days of the Hycsos, or shepherd kings. It is dedicated to the departed mother of the sovereign, "chief Bard of the Sun." The writer, when standing by this splendid memorial, noticed that most of the deeply-cut grooves of hieroglyphics were filled with the mud-cells of a kind of fly. The obelisks of the Druids, rugged and silent, were sometimes of enormous size; that at Locmariaker is said to weigh 260 tons.

Near Heliopolis is the traditional tree, beneath whose shade

Joseph, Mary, and the babe found shelter in the flight to Egypt. Without sufficient faith to reverence it, one cannot but be interested in any relic of superstition. There are, however, awkward facts to be faced before assuming the air of a worshipper. The living sycamore tree now seen in the garden of Heliopolis, and kissed by Christian devotees from many lands, was known to be dead and down in 1672.

There is another variation of the story. The tree was the relic of the Garden of Balsam, or balm of Gilead, the plants of which were sent by the Queen of Sheba to King Solomon, and one afterwards obtained from Jerusalem and carried to Egypt by the *pious* Cleopatra ! Out of the grove but one tree remained when Bakoui was there in 1403. Peter Martyr saw "not the slightest trace" of it in 1403 ; nor did Baumgarten. One tree is said to have recovered (being too profitable an investment for priests), and was mentioned by Leo Africanus, in 1526. Sandys had it pointed out to him in 1610. However, in an excessive inundation of the Nile, during 1615, the tree again perished. But, as it was the identical one in the opening of which the Virgin Mary had concealed herself and child from the pursuers, it could not but be immortal, or subject to resurrection. It is still to be seen, and is still adored.

Those who are curious about such matters will learn, in another work, how the Virgin Mother of the gods in ancient Egypt was hidden in the Divine sycamore. She is still to be seen on the painted walls, and in old papyri, seated amidst the foliage of the holy tree. Religious traditions never die, but re-appear in new dress from time to time.

THE SPHINX.

ALTHOUGH sphinxes were common in Egypt (and not absent from India), were associated with temples, were called *Andro-sphinx*, with human head, *Creo-sphinx*, with ram's head, and *Hieraco-sphinx*, with hawk's head, our present object is the consideration of the Great Sphinx, next the Great Pyramid.

Pliny was told it was the tomb of Amosis, who expelled the Hycsos. Others of the ancients contended that it held the mummy of Rhodope, the rosy-cheeked friend of several Pharaohs. Its mutilated state, say Arab writers, arose from a fanatical sheik, about the year 1379, who broke the nose of the *idol* in his zeal for *Allah*. Abd'allatif wrote, hundreds of years ago, " We see upon the figure a reddish tint and a red varnish. Its mouth has the imprint of grace and beauty." Mr. W. Hamilton, F.R.S., recently asserted that it had once been painted. As to the mouth, its grace and beauty fled when civilised visitors began chipping it away for relics.

Thevenot, the old traveller, recorded a tradition about it, as De Breves has done since. " Authors," he tells us, "report that this Sphinx, as soon as the sun was up, gave responses to anything it was consulted about, and such as go to the pyramid say that the priests conveyed themselves into it (the Sphinx) by the well found in the pyramid, but without any probability, as by search is found; for neither is there any passage discernible in the well, nor is the image hollow. The conjecture, therefore, of the Arabian author seems reasonable, who tells us, that to express the fertility occasioned by the overflowing of the Nile, the Egyptians built this great statue."

Pococke, the English traveller, has left some details of measurement, stating, "The lower part of the neck, or the beginning of the breast, is 33 feet wide; and it is 20 feet from the fore-part of the neck to the back, and thence to the hole in the back it is 75 feet, the hole being 5 feet long, from which to the tail, if I mistake not, it is 30 feet." This somewhat exceeds Pliny's account, which was that it is 113 feet long. The head only appears above the sand at present. A picture in *Harris's Voyages*, about 1705, gives far more of the head than can now be distinguished. The wings, as they are called, behind the ears, are very distinct, as well as the eyes, ears, and chin. Grobert, in 1798, regrets that "the Sphinx is actually very disfigured." Denon then described it thus: "The expression of the head is gentle, gracious, and tranquil; the character of it is African. But the mouth, of which the lips are thick, has a softness in the movement, and a fineness of execution truly admirable; it is flesh and life." Maillet, 180 years ago, saw the broken nose and red paint, and expressed his belief that "this idol was formerly covered by a temple." Dr. Temple-man, 1792, thought that "the *wings* were probably added to the Sphinx, as emblematical of the *fuga temporum*."

Regarded as a female head with the body of a lion, the Sphinx was supposed to represent the constellations *Leo* and *Virgo*. Others saw in the smiling face the attractions of vice, and the after penalty of the claws of the lion. These pretty fancies were dispelled by the discovery of fragments of a beard. Mr. Piazzi Smyth says, "It is a man's face, and had once a huge stone beard." When, through Count Caviglia and Mr. Consul Salt, the sand was cleared away in front, a part of this beard was found fallen between the paws of the lion figure. This clear-ance was an expensive work in 1817. The Arabs made such extensive chippings for talismans that the sand had to be restored quickly to the level.

The French, in 1798, uncovered the back only, but Caviglia revealed the existence of a small temple between the outstretched paws. The height of the Sphinx was found 63 feet, according to one, but 70 is given by Mr. Perring. The length is variously given, up to 177 feet. The whole had been excavated out of the solid rock, except a part of the back and the fore-paws, which are seen cased with hewn stone. The features, doubtless, resembled the king by whom it was erected; as other Andro-sphinxes can, in many cases, be identified by comparison with existing statues. The remains of the royal cap, with the mystic uræus or serpent ornament, may be detected on this one. The boring with iron rods by Colonel Vyse has proved that no hollow exists.

The temple between the paws is clearly of comparatively modern structure. Dr. Richardson reports that in its front " was a granite altar with four horns, one of which remained, and the marks of fire from the burning of incense were visible upon it." A granite slab, 14 feet by 7, is placed against the breast of the Sphinx, bearing the cartouche of the Theban king, Thothmes IV. The eighteenth dynasty is represented in a votive inscription on the miniature temple. A number of other tablets are about the paws in various languages, Greek, and even Latin. Dr. Richardson considered none of them older than the second century. One is a record that a column had been erected near there to the Emperor Nero, who had been present at the temple rites, and had worshipped the sun. One of the Greek legends has been thus rendered by Dr. Young :—

" Thy form stupendous here the gods have placed,
    Sparing each spot of harvest-bearing land ;
And with this mighty work of art have graced
    A rocky isle encumbered once with sand ;
Not that fierce Sphinx which Thebes erewhile laid waste,
    But great Latona's servant, mild and bland ;
Watching that prince beloved who fills the throne
Of Egypt's plain, and calls the Nile his own :
That heavenly monarch who his foes defies ;
Like Vulcan powerful, and like Pallas wise."

Without entering here upon the religious aspect of the Sphinx question, to be treated of elsewhere, one may naturally enquire whether it can have any reference to the pyramids. Mr. Piazzi Smyth declares that, in relation to them, " it lies in a different direction from the great causeway of ancient approach." As Herodotus never so much as mentions its existence, we get no light from him. The ancient Egyptians were too fond of enigmas to leave us any expression of opinion on it.

Situated in front of the Second Pyramid, it was conjectured that its age might date from the builder, King Cephren. Mariette Bey found the name of that monarch on the stele or tablet of Thebes : "in a line," says he, "which further on is almost entirely broken away; a portion of his *Name-Shield*, unfortunately quite isolated, has been still preserved, therefore undoubtedly it had some sort of reference to the builders of the pyramid which is situated behind it." Then, again, Cheops, of the Great Pyramid, has been supposed the author of the Sphinx, though once Dr. Birch imagined it not so old. The discovery of a precious tablet has removed the doubt, and led the distinguished French Curator to say, "The Great Sphinx of the pyramids, after being attributed to Thoutmes IV., then to Chephren, is here cited as anterior to Cheops himself, since it figures as one of the monuments which that prince restored."

Among the triumphs of hieroglyphical reading few can be placed equal to that connected with this wonderful tablet, dug out of a wall, which was found at the foot of the southernmost of the three small pyramids of Gizeh. As M. Auguste Mariette proudly says, "Now we know, by a stone in the Boulaq Museum, that the Sphinx *existed already* when Cheops, second king of the fourth dynasty, ordered the restoration, of which this stone has for its object the consecration of memory." We are the more confounded at such remote antiquity, and are almost disposed to regard the Sphinx with that awe which leads the Arabs now to recognise it as *Abou el Hôl*, the *Father of Terrors*.

Although belonging to the forthcoming or religious part of our subject, something must here be said about the curious so-called "Temple of the Sphinx." Not even the pyramid itself excites more interest and wonder than this edifice recently discovered in the sands near the Sphinx. "It is," according to the learned Renan, "absolutely different from those known elsewhere." Whether temple or tomb, "not an ornament, not a sculpture, not a letter," appeared about it. The statue of King Cephren, with some other figures and tablets, rescued from the well of the building, were evidently thrust down there by the priests in some national struggle or disaster, without connection with the purposes of its erection. One has well characterised the structure as having "a beauty of repose, and an elegance of simplicity."

Mariette Bey inclines to the opinion that it is the most ancient known sepulchre in the world. In exterior and interior there is a resemblance to the *mastaba* of tombs. Its form being that of a *cross* disposes others more readily to believe it a temple, that being the shape of the oldest known religious edifices in the world.

There can be but little doubt that the so-called temple of the Sphinx, and it may be the Sphinx itself, can claim the age of six thousand years.

WHY WAS THE PYRAMID BUILT?

Sir Walter Scott, commonly supposed a man of taste and cultured imagination, spoke of the pyramid as " disagreeable in form, and senseless in utility." A certain writer once remarked of these monuments, " They are nothing at all but heaps of stones." A prosaic Yankee thus recorded his sentiments : " A pyramid is nothing but dollars.—We have got the pyramids in our pockets, and can set them up any day we please."

On the other hand, we have Mr. Gliddon saying, " What monuments on earth have given rise to more fables, speculations, errors, and misconceptions?" This, at any rate, proves the interest they have excited in the minds of men. It is only in our own day that literature and science, not less than poetry and religion, have been directed thither with perfect enthusiasm. To no one man are we so much indebted for the popular feeling in favour of the Great Pyramid, as to Prof. Piazzi Smyth. By making it truly holy ground, by demonstrating, to the satisfaction of many, the divine authorship of the institution, he has surrounded it with a halo it never wore before.

The views entertained as to the object of the erection will now be mentioned.

1. BARRIERS AGAINST THE DESERT SANDS.

This opinion was expressed by M. Fialin de Persigny in 1845, who spoke of "the destination and permanent utility of the pyramids of Egypt and Nubia against the sandy irruptions of the desert."

2. SATAN'S SEAT.

Sir Thomas Browne, who flourished in the Elizabethan age, declares that "these dark caves and mummy repositories are Satan's abodes."

3. IMITATION OF NOAH'S ARK OR TOWER OF BABEL.

Mr. Thomas Yeates, in 1833, wrote, "The Great Pyramid soon followed the Tower of Babel, and had the same common origin." Again, "Whether it was not a copy of the original Tower of Babel? And, moreover, whether the dimensions of these structures were not originally taken from the Ark of Noah?" Elsewhere he has it: "The measures of the Great Pyramid at the base do so approximate to the measures of the Ark of Noah in ancient cubit measure, that I cannot scruple, however novel the idea, to draw a comparison. The form of the Ark was quadrangular, and consisted of equal sides or parallelograms, of which the measures of one is given in three numbers, 300, 50, and 30 cubits." He assures us that it was made for floating only; and that its four sides were each of three stories to accommodate the large number of persons required to look after so many animals for a whole year.

4. FILTERING RESERVOIRS.

A Swedish philosopher gave it as his opinion that pyramids were simply contrivances for purifying the water of the muddy Nile, which would pass through their passages.

5. TO PLEASE THE WOMEN.

Mr. Gable informs his readers that, as pyramids have no access, "it appears not that the founders of them had any such laudable design of transmitting to posterity scientific specimens," as some had supposed ; "hence they appear to have been erected for no geometrical purpose." Having, however, ascertained (how, he says not) that they were raised by those, "who, after their intermarriages with the daughters of men, became, not only degenerate despisers of useful knowledge, but altogether abandoned to luxury,"—it is not surprising that he should have found out that it was to please these women, who requested the sons of God to employ their leisure after that fashion.

6. THE QUEEN OF SHEBA'S GIFTS.

Orientals may be excused telling romantic tales of this romantic lady traveller ; but Mr. Wathen, in 1842, said that "the offerings of the Queen of Sheba are now beheld in the indestructible masses of the pyramids."

7. JOSEPH'S GRANARIES.

Benjamin of Toledo, the travelled Jew of the Middle Ages, advanced this opinion, which he had gathered in the East. Vossius heard somehow that the Pharaoh had "magazined" a great quantity of wheat there. The Monk Fidelis says the same. An American writer, in 1876, must have astonished and shocked some folks, by his bold assertion, learnt somewhere or somehow, that "according to the hypothesis of Prof. Piazza Smyth, the object of the Great Pyramid was to convert it into a granary in time of famine" (!).

Maundeville, about 1330, got the complete story. "The Gernares of Joseph," says he, "that he lete make, for to kepe the greynes for the peril of the dere zeres. Thei ben (are) made of ston, full welle made of masonnes craft, of the whiche two ben merveyllouse grete and hye, and to these ne ben not so gret; and every Gerner hath a zate (gate) for to entre withinne, a lytille

highe fro the Erthe, for the lond is wasted and fallen sithe the
Gerners were made. And withinne thei ben alle fulle of ser-
pentes. And aboven the Gerners withouten ben many Scriptures
of dyverse languages. And sum men seyn (say) that thei ben
sepultures of grete lordes that weren sometyme; but that is not
trewe; for alle the comoun rymour and speche is of alle the peple
there, both fer and nere, that thei ben the Gerners of Joseph.
And so fynden thei in here Scriptures and in here cronycles.
On that other partie, zif thei weren sepultures thei sholden not
ben voyd withinne. For yee may well knowe that tombes and
sepultures ne ben not made of such gretnesse, ne of such
highnesse."

8. DISPLAY OF ROYAL DESPOTISM.

Aristotle, while admitting this motive, considered the priests
had persuaded the king to undertake the work, in order to find
employment for the idle. Pliny deemed it proper for a great
conqueror to keep his captives busy. Greaves, the Oxford Professor, 250 years ago, goes into the question. "But why," he
says, "the Egyptian kings should have been at so vast an
expense in the building of these pyramids is an enquiry of a
higher nature. Aristotle makes them to have been the workes of
tyranny; and Pliny conjectures that they built them partly out
of ostentation, and partly out of state policy, by keeping the
people in employment, to divert them from mutinies and rebel-
lions." Sandys thought it was "for feare lest such infinite
wealth should corrupt their suc·essors, and dangerous idlenesse
beget in the subject a desire for innovation." He gives a rude
translation from Lucian :—

> " When high pyramides do grace
> The ghosts of Ptolomies lewd race."

Mariette Bey is indignant at this supposition, exclaiming, "They are not monuments of the vain ostentation of kings." Hekekyan Bey shrewdly remarks: "It is well known that a tyrant scarcely ever completes a work left unfinished by his predecessor. It is evident that these pyramids were national undertakings; their plan and execution were decided after mature deliberation; laws were passed, and revenues provided, to carry out the public decision by the executive authorities." M. Dufeu adds his affirmation, that, "far from being the works of the pride and despotism of Pharaohic kings, they are, on the contrary, testimonies of their exalted wisdom, and of the profound knowledge of their colleges of priests."

The Rev. E. B. Zincke has a practical suggestion. "In those days," says he, "labour could not be bottled up." Egypt was so fertile, and men's wants were then so few, that surplus labour was available, and much food, from taxes in kind, accumulated in royal hands. Although the pyramid was of no earthly use, "still," thought he, "it was of as much benefit to the man who built it as leaving the surplus labour and food he had at his disposal, and the valuables he had in his treasury unused would be."

9. PRESERVATION OF LEARNING FROM THE EXPECTED DELUGE.

It having been revealed by the antediluvian astrologers that a great flood was coming, the pyramid was built to preserve the memory of then-existing learning. We are indebted to Arabian authors for this interesting tradition, which has several variations. Firouzabadi was not very clear upon the subject. He speaks of the erection "by Edris, to preserve there the sciences, and prevent their destruction by the Deluge; or by Sinan ben-almo-

schalshal, or by the first men, when informed by observation of
the stars of the coming Deluge ; or to preserve medicines, magic,
and talismans."

Murtadi is another authority. He wrote in 992, at Tihe in
Arabia, or in the year of our Lord 1584, says one. The work
was translated in 1672. This is the story :—

" There was a king named Saurid, the son of Sahaloc, 300
years before the Deluge, who dreamed one night that he saw
the earth overturned with its inhabitants, the men cast down
on their faces, the stars falling out of the heavens, and striking
one against the other, and making horrid and dreadful cries
as they fell. He thereupon awoke much troubled, and related
not his dream to anybody, and was satisfied in himself that
some great accident would happen in the world. A year after
he dreamed again that he saw the fixed stars come down to the
earth in the form of white birds, which carried men away, and
cast them between two great mountains, which almost joined together and covered them; and then the bright, shining stars
became dark and were eclipsed. He thereupon awaked, and
extremely astonished, and entered into the Temple of the Sun,
and beset himself to bathe his cheeks and to weep. Next morn-
ing he ordered all the princes of the priests, and magicians of
all the provinces of Egypt, to meet together ; which they did to
the number of 130 priests and soothsayers, with whom he went
and related to them his dream, which they found very important
and of great consequence, and the interpretation they gave of
it was that some very great accident would happen in the
world.

" Among others, the priest Aclimon, who was the greatest of
all, and resided chiefly in the king's Court, said thus to him :—

'Sir, your dream is admirable, and I myself saw another about a year since which frightened me very much, and which I have not revealed to any one.' 'Tell me what it was,' said the king. 'I dreamt,' said the priest, 'that I was with your Majesty on the top of the mountain of fire, which is in the midst of Emsos, and that I saw the heaven sink down below its ordinary situation, so that it was near the crown of our heads, covering and surrounding us, like a great basin turned upside down; that the stars were intermingled among men in diverse figures; that the people implored your Majesty's succour, and ran to you in multitudes as their refuge; that you lifted up your hands above your head, and endeavoured to thrust back the heaven, and keep it from coming down so low; and that I, seeing what your Majesty did, did also the same. While we were in that posture, extremely affrighted, methought we saw a certain part of heaven opening, and a bright light coming out of it; that afterwards the sun rose out of the same place, and we began to implore his assistance; whereupon he said thus to us: "The heaven will return to its ordinary situation when I shall have performed three hundred courses." I thereupon awaked extremely affrighted.'

"The priest having thus spoken, the king commanded them to take the height of the stars, and to consider what accident they portended. Whereupon they declared that they promised first the Deluge, and after that fire. Then he commanded pyramids should be built, that they might remove and secure in them what was of most esteem in their treasuries, with the bodies of the kings, and their wealth, and the aromatic roots which served them, and that they should write their wisdom upon them, that the violence of the water might not destroy it."

This is a version of the story of Shem engraving the learning of the old world upon two pillars—Jachin and Boaz, Pillars of Hercules.

Ibn Abd Alhokm is the chronicler of a tradition, also, of a like import with that retailed by Murtadi. The translation is an old one. The Arabian historian thus discourses :—

"The greatest part of chronologers agree that he which built the pyramids was Saurid Ibn Salhouk, King of Egypt, who lived 300 years before the Flood. The occasion of this was because he saw in his sleep that the whole earth was turned over, with the inhabitants of it, the men lying upon their faces, and the stars falling down and striking one another with a terrible noise; and being troubled with this, he concealed it. Then, after this, he saw the fixed stars falling to the earth, in the similitude of white fowl, and they snatched up men and carried them between two great mountains, and these mountains closed upon them, and the shining stars were made dark. And he awoke with great fear, and assembled the chief priests of all the provinces of Egypt, 130 priests, the chief of them being Almamon. He related the whole matter to them, and they took the altitude of the stars, and made their prognostications, and they foretold a deluge. The king said, 'Will it come to our country?' They answered, 'Yes, and will destroy it.' And there remained a certain number of years to come, and he commanded in the mean space to build the pyramids, and that a vault (or cistern) should be made, into which the river Nile should enter, whence it should run into the countries of the west, and into the land Al-Said.

"And he filled them (the pyramids) with talismans, and with strange things, and with riches and treasures, and the like. He engraved in them all things that were told him by wise men, as, also, all profound sciences. The names of alakakirs, the uses and hurts of them, the science of astrology and of arithmetic, of geometry and physic. All these may be interpreted by him who knows their characters and language. After he had given orders for this building, they cut out great columns and wonderful stones. They fetched massy stones from the Ethiopians, and made with them the foundations of the three pyramids, fastening them together with lead and iron. (?) They built the gates of them 40 cubits under-ground, and they made the height of the pyramids 100 royal cubits, which are 500 of ours in these times. He also made each side of the pyramids 100 royal cubits. In the beginning of this building was a fortunate horoscope. After that he had finished it he covered it with coloured satin (marble) from the top to the bottom, and he appointed a solemn festival, at which were present all the inhabitants of his kingdom. Then he built in the Western Pyramid thirty treasuries, filled with store of riches and utensils, and with signatures made with precious stones, and with instruments of iron, and vessels of earth, and with a *mes* which rots not, and with glass that might be bent and yet not broken, and with strange spells, and with several kinds of alkakirs (query *alkalis*), single and double, and with deadly poisons, and with other things besides. He made, also, in the East Pyramid divers celestial spheres and stars, and what they severally operate in their aspects; and perfumes which are to be used to them, and the books which treat of these matters.

"He put, also, in the Coloured Pyramid (the *third*) the commentaries of the priests in chests of block marble, and with every priest a book, in which were the wonders of his profession, and of his actions, and of his nature, and what was done in his time, and what is, and what shall be, from the beginning of time to the end of it. He placed in every pyramid a treasurer. The treasurer of the Westerly Pyramid was a statue of marble stone, standing upright with a lance, and upon his head a serpent writhed. He that came near it, and stood still, the serpent bit him of one side, and writhed round about his throat and killed him, and then returned to his place. He made the treasurer of the East Pyramid an idol of black agate, his eyes open and shining, sitting upon a throne with a lance. When any looked upon him he heard on one side of him a voice which took away his senses, so that he fell prostrate upon his face, and ceased not till he died. He made the treasurer of the Coloured Pyramid a statue of stone called Albut, sitting. He which looked toward it was drawn by the statue till he stuck to it, and could not be separated from it till such time as he died."

So much for the Arab yarn of the pyramids before the Flood.

10. TOMB OF THE KING.

Herodotus, describing the building of the pyramid by Philitis, says that "Cheops ordered Philitis to prepare him a tomb." But many, seeing the pit there, and erroneously thinking it a well, ask with Mr. Yeates, "What have the dead to do with wells of water? Water is not for the dead, but the living." A Syrian writer, of the ninth century, observed, "They are not granaries of Joseph, as some say, but mausoleums erected upon the tombs of ancient kings." The Rev. Mr. Zincke, who positively asserts that "every pyramid in Egypt was intended for a tomb," is of the conviction that the very word means a *mound* or cairn; he therefore talks of the Aryans who "built the cairn of Gizeh." Servius is clearly of that mind when he writes, "With the ancients, noble men were buried either under mountains or in mountains, whence the custom came that over the dead either pyramids were made or huge cairns erected."

Professional architects generally take the tomb side. Thus Mr. Fergusson decides upon it, and Mr. Guilt says the pyramids are "sepulchral monuments, whether or not the bodies of the monarchs were ever deposited in them." We have remaining on a tablet the prayer of a certain priest, Ahra, that his son would make his name live again, whilst he reposed in his pyramid, or tomb. Chevalier Bunsen, who paid such attention to Egyptian antiquities, has no doubt but that all pyramids were "exclusively gigantic covers of rocky tombs." The .word of M. Maillet is justified, that, "with regard to the design they had of securing their bodies from any insult, they could not have contrived more certain means for succeeding in it."

Mariette Bey, who for explorative ardour rivals the energetic Belzoni himself, is an advocate for the tomb theory. This is his language : "With regard to the use to which the pyramids were destined, it is to do violence to all that we know of Egypt, to all that archæology teaches us of the monumental customs of that country, to see them any other thing than tombs." Again, "tombs, massive, full, *everywhere stopped*, even in their passages, most carefully, without windows, without doors, without exterior opening." He alludes to the care taken to throw seekers off the scent. He compares tombs with pyramids, showing the devices in both sorts to deceive attempting violaters of mummy-homes.

An account of an Egyptian tomb is necessary to enable the reader to form a judgment upon the question.

In case some should suppose the tombs remaining there to be of more modern date than the Giant Pyramids, it must be borne in mind that Mariette Bey has distinctly laid it down that every pyramid is in the middle of a cemetery. And M. Chabas writes of the Necropolis of Gizeh, with its vast collection of massive tombs : "A certain number of these tombs have been constructed at the same time as the Great Pyramid, and finished *before* that colossal monument." Lepsius got what he calls an official almanac of the Court of the Kings Cheops and Cephren, the tombs giving so many names of their officers. Our own Dr. Birch adds this striking testimony : "The tombs around the Great Pyramid are those of the princes and other members of the family or time of Khufu" (builder of that pyramid). M. Grobert affirms, "I believe these grottoes more ancient than even the pyramids." Lepsius opened a hundred of them, and was satisfied of this assumed antiquity. Mariette Bey has been able to show that the funeral fields of both Gizeh and Saqqarah were absolutely closed as early as the time of Teta, king of the sixth dynasty, a hundred years or so after the building of the Great Pyramid. He has unearthed the splendid tomb of a grandson of Snefrou, king of the third dynasty, besides several Mastabas of the age of Snefrou, and declares that the period of some "ascends even to the predecessors of the founders of the Great Pyramid." Renan adds, "The tombs, so numerous in the sands of Sakkara and at the foot of the pyramids, are all dated from the first six dynasties."

If all the above statements are not arguments enough to prove that tombs exist which are at least as old as the pyramid, we are now assured by such an authority as Lepsius, the first of

German Egyptologists, that there are at least sixty inedited tombs at Gizeh and Saqqarah, which are of the *first dynasty*— or far more than 6000 years old.

What, then, is an ancient Egyptian tomb?

There are three parts essentially different. First there is the *Mastaba*, or exterior chapel; then, the pit near it; and, below, the subterranean chamber for the corpse. The body was taken down the pit into the tomb proper, and laid in the sarcophagus there. The pit was then effectually closed up and all communication cut off.

There are whole streets of stone tombs, the funeral chapels of which only are to be seen. Though of stone, Mr. Fergusson says they show "evident symptoms of having been borrowed from a wooden original." He styles these Mastabas "truncated pyramids." One has been discovered 400 feet long. One to the west of the valley is 320 feet. But in the earliest tombs the chamber is so small that few can stand in it. The plan has the *form of a cross*. Many tombs later than the fourth dynasty possess more than one chamber, with more careful orientation. Though yellow brick tombs prevailed during the first four dynasties, the fifth has none but stone ones. The Mastabas, in general appearance, are like unfinished pyramids, but only in the inclined sides.

The Mastabas of Gizeh are more uniform and symmetrical than those near Memphis. "They are ranged like a chessboard," says M. Auguste Mariette, "with their squares uniformly elongated towards the north." Generally 8 yards high, there are many of them 50 yards long by 25 yards wide. In the sixth dynasty the roof is vaulted. The entrance is from the east.

The *pit* is never round. Though mostly in the middle of the great axis of the Mastaba, there is no connection with the upper chapel. To reach the orifice, in many cases, one has to mount to the platform of the Mastaba.

Dr. Lepsius gives an interesting account of a tomb-discovery. He explored first the Mastaba, a noble apartment 70 feet long, 14 wide, and 15 high. On the walls, as usual, there was the written and pictorial history of the individual buried beneath. The tomb, which was on the west side of the Great Pyramid, proved to belong to Prince Merhet, of the time of Cheops. The learned gentleman writes : "It is more than probable that Merhet was a son of Chufu" (Cheops). He is styled "Superintendent of buildings" to that monarch. "One may, therefore," says he, "conjecture that *he himself superintended the building of the largest pyramid.*" Lepsius descended, after much difficulty, the heretofore closed-up pit, and found at a depth of *sixty* feet the hypogeum, or sepulchre chamber, and the sarcophagus, or real tomb.

A wonderful discovery awaited him. After being unmolested since the interment, 6000 years ago, the relics of the mighty dead were revealed. It was, doubtless, with feelings of pride and gratification that he afterwards wrote, "I have carefully preserved the venerable remains of the skull of the ancient prince of the House of Cheops, which I found in his mortuary chamber."

The sarcophagus contained the coffin. The earliest coffin, or mummy-case, that ever reached England was described by Dr. Perry, 1743. He who has seen the richly-carved alabaster sarcophagus of the nineteenth dynasty, in Sir John Soane's

Museum, Lincoln's Inn, especially if favoured with a description from the lips of the octogenarian librarian and curator, Mr. Bonomi, of hieroglyphic artistic renown, will have a high conception of the symbolic religion of the ancient Egyptians. But the observer of the more ancient funeral repositories would have more simplicity of style before him. One of the twelfth dynasty, an era of great advancement and high culture, is described by M. Rougé as " cut with great precision, but is only adorned by a simple hieroglyphical legend," naming the individual and his occupation. But ascending still higher, to the age of the pyramids, and regarding the sarcophagus of the monarch who raised the Third Pyramid of Gizeh, we recognise good workmanship, but no fanciful adornment. The learned Frenchman writes :—
" That of the King Menkeres (fourth dynasty) presents the appearance of a little edifice. It was *not decorated by any figure :* simple architectural lines, disposed with infinite taste, alone compose its ornamentation."

There is no space to devote to a discourse on ancient tombs, or attention would have been drawn to the highly interesting explorations of Dr. Schliemann at Troy and Mycenæ. The tombs of Atreus and of King Alyattes are well known to readers ; the platform of the latter, at Sardis, is even now 3700 feet round. Tumuli exist in Asia of enormous proportions. One in Afghanistan has a boundary of 1800 feet. The Topes of India are suggestive. The mound-builders of America have left one monument in Illinois which is 2000 feet in circumference. The *Galgals* of Brittany, and the one-chambered or several-chambered *Barrows* of Britain, are also massive and gigantic memorials of the dead. The *Teocalli* of Mexico were equally devoted to purposes of burial.

The so-called Temple of the Sphinx, near the pyramid, has been looked on simply as a tomb; and, if so, is the most ancient, and one of the most costly and magnificent in the world. Mariette Bey thus speaks of it :—"The exterior appearance is, we must declare, rather that of a tomb. Further, the monument can present itself to the visitor as a Mastaba, hardly greater than those which one finds, for example, at Abousir and at Saqqarah. In the interior, the chamber shows six superposed niches, which have the air of having been constructed, as those of the Third Pyramid, and of the Mastabat-el-Faroun, to receive mummies."

Turning now to the Great Pyramid, what do we notice—apart from certain peculiarities—but the same arrangements for the burial of a body as occur in an ordinary ancient tomb? The simplicity, spoken of in connection with the sarcophagus of the builder of the Third Pyramid, is apparent in the First. The King's Chamber, with its so-called sarcophagus, was no more the mortuary chamber than the Mastaba of the tomb. The real burial-room was below the surface, and at the end of a pit. That pit is to be seen inside the Great Pyramid, and that mortuary space is extant as the Subterranean Chamber. That the latter was found without an occupant proves no more than the tenantless tombs.

But it will be asked, what answers to the Mastaba—the Chapel? Inside that open and accessible place, with a doorway in the east, apparent to any passer-by, the friends of the deceased could assemble for the anniversary rites. There, too, they could read the story of the departed. Where is the parallel of this in the Great Pyramid?

Only two chambers, called the King's and the Queen's, have

been revealed. There is reason to think others are still hidden. But they, in their naked aspect, with no sculptured memorial and no painting, though partaking of the simplicity of the last home of King Menkeres, were never designed for observation, could never have been entered by friends and relatives, but were from the first most carefully blocked up and secreted. The temples once standing before each pyramid served as chapels.

11. A STANDARD OF WEIGHTS AND MEASURES.

This is, perhaps, the most important and practical issue from pyramid enquiry. One question is—does the building indicate any special standard? The other question follows—does that measure proceed from a scientific basis?

Opinions upon the state of ancient learning range between absurd depreciation and unreasonable exaltation. Still there can be no question but that the tendency of modern thought is to value increasingly the results of ancient study. But we, as Europeans, have so prided ourselves upon our mathematical skill, and the approximate perfection of our methods of calculation, as to suppose it highly improbable, to say the least, that men who lived in Egypt 6000 years before Newton and Laplace could know more than the rudiments.

Yet, what says M. Gosselin in his *Systematic and Positive Geography of the Ancients* ? It is this : " The itinerary measures of the ancients are more exact than is thought. In comparing them with the plan of the earth, as it is known to us, it is often difficult, sometimes even impossible, to decide if the errors, which are fancied to be observed in these itineraries, ought to be rejected upon the report of the ancients rather than upon the imperfection of our actual knowledge."

But M. A. Dufeu, the learned author of *Decouverté de l'age et de la véritable destination des Quatre Pyramides de Gizeh, principalement de la Grande Pyramide*, has these weighty remarks : " An extreme precision, a thing at which the mind stands truly confounded, appears to have presided at the operations and geodesic calculations of the ancient Egyptians; and it seems that modern science has not yet been able to rise to that height to which that ever-memorable people had already arrived." The testimony of this French *savant* is thus confirmatory of the supposed extravagant estimate of Prof. Piazzi Smyth, if not recognising with him a special inspiration.

Although the Edinburgh Professor is credited with the fatherhood of the idea that the pyramid contains a standard of measure, it will be seen that he has but accepted the theory of those before him. Yet he has done much. By the exercise of mathematical skill he has developed the theory; and by the energy and enthusiasm of his appeals to the public he has given it an interest and a popularity never realised before.

But that which has intensified the interest is the excitation of the marvellous in man by the announcement that this said standard was an ordinance from heaven—*a gift from God*. By bringing the religious faculty into the arena of discussion, a vast increase of force has been acquired. Argue as philosophers will upon materialism, they are confronted with the practical reply, from all the ages, of the *intuitive* in humanity. There is a something at the back of all that cannot be accounted for by the rude logic of facts. There is in man a perception, however obscure and ill-defined, of spiritual existence, that sometimes comes with such power as to sweep away all dykes of reason and philosophy, and stir to the very depths the hearts of nations as of individuals. The mass are, and perhaps ever will be, governed more or less by a feeling of the supernatural. The alliance, therefore, of religion with the pyramid idea of measurement at once lifted the theory from the field of abstract, scientific enquiry into the domain of sympathetic belief. So long as Hindoo and European casuists squabbled over *free-will*, the doctrine never got beyond the schools; it was quite otherwise when it sharpened the sword of the Saracens, and nerved the arm of Cromwell's Ironsides.

But let us, for the present, put aside the supernatural prop of the theory, and take a prosaic view of the pyramid standard of measure.

When Prof. Greaves, 240 years ago, took his ten-feet rule, accurately divided into thousandths of a foot, and laid it upon the hoary monument by the Nile, he was not a little astonished at the result.

On his return to the Oxford Observatory he published a series of letters. The work—" printed by G. Sawbridge, at the Three Flower-de-Luces, in Little Britain "—was entitled, *Origine and Antiquity of our English weights and measures discovered by their near agreement with such standards that are now found in one of the Egyptian Pyramides.*

In his preface to the *Skilful Reader*, he says : " The standards in this pyramid, so nearly agreeing with our perfect English measures, and with those of the antient Persians, Greeks, and Romans, deserve the consideration of the learned, as being in all likelyhood introductory to the discovery of other matters of greater importance."

In agreement with the spirit of those Puritan times, not less than our own, he deals largely with Scripture, and discusses Hebrew cubits, baths, &c. He concludes that the pyramid cubit was 21·875 inches, or 21$\frac{7}{8}$ inches.

Naturally he was most attracted toward the sarcophagus, or *tomb* as he calls it, seeing there a resemblance to the Jewish laver. The Bible represents several lavers before the altar of the second temple; but, though Josephus speaks of the first laver being a hemisphere, the Old Testament adds no confirmatory testimony. Mr. Greaves has these observations on the coffer: "We shall find that every dimension of the tomb's cavity is the axis of a sphere, within whose hemisphere such an inscribed polygone is a standard for some antient measure of capacity; for which cause I conjecture that this figure of a vessel in old times was well known, and seems to be the same with that of the *laver*, in which the priests of those days were used to wash."

Sir Isaac Newton, both as a mathematician and a religious man, took much interest in the Oxford astronomer's speculations.

He wrote a work in Latin upon "The sacred cubit of the Jews, and the cubits of the several nations; in which, from the dimensions of the greatest Egyptian Pyramid, as taken by Mr. John Greaves, the ancient cubit of Memphis is determined."

He was much struck with the fact that, among other convincing measurements, the banks or benches in the Grand Gallery were 1·717 feet broad, and 1·717 feet deep; "that is," says he, "in breadth and depth one cubit. Who will, therefore, imagine that so many dimensions, not at all depending upon each other, should correspond by mere chance with the length of the cubit assigned by us?" But he clearly inclines to a belief that his

$20\frac{1}{2}$ inch cubit was preceded by one of greater length, which may have approximated to 25 inches.

M. Pancton distinctly deserves the honour of the astronomical idea of Egyptian measurement. In 1780 he found the base, 8754 inches, was a five-hundredth portion of a degree of meridian. Well might M. de l'Isle declare that theory of his learned friend to be " one of the principal labours of the human mind."

M. Jomard, in Egypt during 1798—9, comes next in order of time. He was amazed to find the sarcophagus so nearly agree with the newly-declared French *mètre*, and suspected that the former system was based upon astronomical data like the new one. He boldly avowed that " no one can any longer affirm that the idea of invariable measures belongs only to the moderns." He even goes so far as to say, " The history of the sciences demonstrates that the moderns have made several of these measures with much less precision than the ancients." This is exactly the principle contended for by Mr. Piazzi Smyth, who holds the ancient Egyptian mode was more philosophically correct than that of the French metric system.

The French savant of 1799 laid down the principle that the sarcophagus did reveal a system of measures. And although his rule was not correct, he hit upon the cubit idea; " sacred," he says, " and the object of worship with the Egyptian people." From the *box* he learns that " the cube root of a quantity composed of one forty-eighth of the solid resulting from the three exterior dimensions which had been given by the art of the workmen, and of the twelfth part of the solid contents of its interior, is equal to the *Nilometric cubit.*"

He thus upheld the dignity of the sarcophagus :—

"Can it be compared to the sarcophagi of these royal tombs, and has it ever had their destination? This same vessel,—was it a tomb, an image, or was it even a sort of particular vase, having no other object than to receive the mummy of a prince? To admit the supposition that such may have been really enclosed there, would it not be to abandon the witness of Herodotus, who said in formal and positive terms that the place of the king's sepulchre was in an island formed by a canal, and executed in the subterranean passages dug in the rock of the pyramid? And has not Diodorus declared that each of the two kings who built the Great Pyramids was buried there, and that their bodies were put in secret places? It is, then, not at all proved that the pretended King's Chamber had ever enclosed the body."

The Rev. Thomas Gabb, in 1806, gave some interesting tales about the pyramids, and clearly forestalled the present advocates of the measurement theory. He remarks, however, "the very incongruities discovered in dimensions recorded by Vitruvius, Pliny, and Herodotus, in the acceptation of any of the monumental feet, had long since convinced me these authors must have made their calculations by a foot-measure very different from those of the Greek foot published in our tables." He concludes the Egyptian foot, or *cubit* of Herodotus, to be 8·7553 inches, nearly 8¾.

He contends for the *Centesm* standard of measure. The box was "never intended," he thinks, "for a sepulchral monument," as it indicates one-hundredth part of the base of the pyramid. "The founder of this surprising pile," says he, "whoever he may have been, caused that excavated chest to be deposited where it stands, and whence it could not be taken away, as a perpetual criterion whereby, without actual measurement, the exact size of the base might always be known."

Further, he writes, "Copies of which standard chest were, no doubt, dispersed over Egypt and its dependencies; and that brought by Lord Cavan from Alexandria, measured without the astragals at the ends, is the *same in length as that in the pyramid*, as declared to me by Mr. Hay, of Portsea, who measured it on board the vessel while it remained in Portsmouth harbour." This was 10 Egyptian feet, like the coffer, or 10×8.7553 inches. He held that a cubit was $2\frac{1}{2}$ pyramid feet, or 1.824 feet. A degree near the equator would thus be 500,000 pyramid feet.

Count Caviglia, who took up his abode for a time in Davison's uncomfortable chamber, dwelt more upon the mystical than the mathematical exponents of the pyramid.

Mr. Wild, C. E., of Zurich, published in 1850 some marvellous results of his calculations. He assumes that not the Great Pyramid alone, but the other pyramids of Gizeh, in relation, not only indicate a standard measure, which he assumes to be the Memphis one of 20, not 25 inches, but that that cubit has definite reference to astronomical data. His work appeared as a letter to Lord Brougham.

To Mr. John Taylor, of Gower Street, London, are we most deeply indebted. His work of 1856—*The Great Pyramid: why was it built, and who built it ?*—set Mr. Piazzi Smyth to work, and provoked the subsequent interesting discussion. He brought out old revelations, and made known new. He contended for the cubit of 25 inches as the sacred one, and as being a ten-millionth part of the earth's semi-polar axis.

He repeats the language of Greaves and Jomard, saying, " The porphyry coffer in the King's Chamber in the Great Pyramid was intended to be a standard measure of capacity and weight for all nations." English measures were founded thereon, as the coffer held four quarters of our corn-table. "When," said he, " we find in so complicated a series of figures as that which the measures of the Great Pyramid and of the earth require for their expression, *round numbers* present themselves, or such as leave no remainders, we may be sure that we have arrived at primitive measures." Thus he points out that a pyramid inch, which is 1·00099 English, will be exactly one five hundred millionth part of the axis of the earth. A cubit he puts at 25 inches. The Karnac cubit and the coffer, he says, "are irresistible proofs of an identity of measure existing from 3000 to 4000 years ago."

But while he shows that the cube root of the contents of the coffer is the length of the Karnac cubit, he puzzles us with the affirmation that the cubit before the Flood was 24·90 inches, but 25 inches *after* that event; and yet that both were inspired! He accounts for this most satisfactorily to himself, though perhaps not so conclusively to men of science, by assuming that the Deluge exercised so disastrous an effect upon the world —though geologists fail to discover a single material evidence of that Flood at all—that the diameter is less by nearly thirty-seven miles than it was before the ark of Noah was seen to rest upon Mount Ararat.

Hekekyan Bey, in 1863, declared that the "king's stone," as he calls it, was " deposited by the Arions in the sanctuary of the First Pyramid, as a record of their standard metric measure." Prof. Piazzi Smyth brought to the enquiry unquestioned scientific ability, singular tenacity, tremendous energy, exalted enthusiasm, and orthodox piety. The combination is a singularly rare one, and at once placed him as leader of a devoted, intelligent, and numerous party. We may judge of the strength of his convictions, or his haughty defiance of objectors, from the fact that he publicly renounced his fellowship with the Royal Society when that learned body failed to recognise his theory.

Still, all who love the old pyramid will not only thank Mr. Smyth for the light he has shone on their path, but highly esteem the man so loyally attached to their common centre of interest.

Mr. Smyth seeks to enforce the arguments of Mr. Taylor. He identifies pyramid measures with Bible ones, and is pleased to find that these "still preserve some very recognisable traces." He contends that the Great Pyramid is unlike others; they are *Epimethean* and thriftless, while that is *Promethean*, of heaven-born origin. Instead of being a tomb, it is but the covering of a standard for measure. Such a constructed vessel as the coffer, filled with water, kept at uniform temperature by solid walls and efficient ventilation, must be a reliable one for weight as well as measure.

As a standard, the coffer must be for inspection and reference. Copies of it, exposed to mischances of all sorts, must need checks, and require to be brought to the original and tested by it. There is no sense in having a standard, especially a Divinely-authorised standard, without it could be seen from time to time, and made available for the purpose of correcting ordinary weights and measures. The concealment, absolute and total concealment of it, would be an anomaly, an absurdity. Rulers could establish metrical systems without reference to it, or in ignorance of it. The very intention of revelation is conveyed in the term *revelation*. That which cannot be revealed, even if existent, could hardly be termed a revelation.

Mr. Piazzi Smyth is so conscious of this that he dwells upon it. "The King's Chamber," he tells his readers, "was ventilated in the most admirable manner by the 'air-channels' discovered by Colonel Howard Vyse; evidently so that *men might come from time to time and look on and deal with that open granite trough, and live, and not die.*"

He is perfectly right. If it were really intended, by special inspiration or not, as a standard, then it must be accessible. But what are the facts? Simply, and he himself affirms the same in another place, that immediately upon the completion of the pyramid the King's Chamber was blocked up so securely that not till force was applied by the Caliph, in 820, was it ever entered again.

What, then, is the natural deduction? Is it not that, though measurements of the pyramid-coffer were agreeable to what was *then* a *recognised standard*, and symbolically represented recognised ideas, yet the coffer *itself was not intended by its constructors as a reference-standard.*

But it is time that we look more closely into the measurements more or less affected by the lines in the pyramid.

Those found by Greaves, and described by Newton, are termed by the Edinburgh Professor "the profane measures of the Egyptian people;" inasmuch as they dealt with other calculations than those regarded as Divine, like the sacred cubit of 25 inches. Yet Newton refers to a "proper and principal cubit" of the Israelites. After various trials he gets something between 24 and 26 inches, but does not decide upon anything. He notes a cubit received through Mersennus and a knight of St. Michael's, supposed to be a Jewish secret, and which was 24·91 inches. He thus clearly distinguishes two sorts of cubits.

By another interesting method the 25, or its double measure, is obtained. The transverse height of the passage is 44·8 inches; but at the angle of 26° 18' this becomes the vertical height, 50 inches. "Thus," says the professor, "a measure in which the Egyptian workmen could see nothing more than some of their profane cubits and palms, is converted by means of that angle into another indication of the great linear standard of the pyramid, or the one ten-millionth of the earth's axis of rotation."

The cubit question, though dry enough, has its points of interest. Mr. Smyth says that Moses adopts the sacred or 25 inch cubit, while the profane Egyptian, in that day, was less. He says that "we may with perfect safety and hierologist support regard the length of 20·7 inches as the veritable hereditary measure of the Egyptians." How, then, did Moses get the other? He believes, from the pyramid. "In the Great Pyramid," he says, "we have found enshrined and sealed up, from those pre-Abrahamic to these latter days, that identical sacred measure-space of the Jews."

As he states elsewhere that the building "had remained sealed in all its more important divisions from the date of its foundation up to an advanced period of the Christian dispensation," Moses could never have looked at the coffer. But, as an admitted Egyptian priest, and married to the daughter of the high-priest of the sun, at the temple of On or Heliopolis, he may have been admitted to a knowledge of some of the mysteries of Egypt. If so, no adept can charge him with having published the secrets, though Mr. Smyth believes he retained in the ark the secret of measure. Anyhow, he nowhere reveals that secret, any more than others, though, like the Egyptians, typifying ideas by numbers and things.

Some have supposed that Moses got his knowledge when he fled to—what had been for ages before the sacred mount of the Arab race—Sinai. There, from some venerable priest, he may have got the sacred cubit. The desert men, Divinely inspired to conquer Egypt, and to build a pyramid for the standard measure, according to Mr. Piazzi Smyth, retreated afterwards to their Arabian wilderness, and, doubtless, carried there some of the old teaching.

After all, it may be asked, why take 25 as a sacred cubit? Messrs. Taylor and Smyth contend for 5 being the test number of the pyramid. Five squared makes the required number. Out of a variety of different measurements, Mr. Smyth professes to take a mean of 9; yet that is not his 25·07, but 25·29. Taylor's cubit was presumed to be the ten-millionth of the radius of the earth, and 25·025. Sir John Herschel recognises such a cubit as probably existing among the Jews.

But, however pretty the theory, is it according to facts? Can the cubit of 25·025 be found in the pyramid? If not, it is in vain we speak of the 25 pyramid inches' cubit being one ten-millionth part of the polar semi-axis. Sir Edmund Beckett, among the first of British architects who has given some attention to pyramid matters, distinctly says that Mr.

Smyth's 25 inch cubit is *not* to be found in the building.   Here
are his conclusions :—

" It is not worth while to say more of those theories here than
to mention the *unlucky fact* that neither the Jewish sacred cubit
of 25 inches, which is the imaginary basis of them all, nor any
multiple of it, is to be found in a single one of all Mr. Smyth's
multitude of measurements, except two evidently accidental
multiples of it in the diagonals of two of the four corner sockets
in the rock, which are not square, and could never have been
seen again after the pyramid was built if the superstructure had
not been broken up and stolen, which was probably the last
thing that Cheops or his architect expected.   The idea that a
building was designated to perpetuate a measure which *it*
exhibits absolutely nowhere !"

His conclusion is emphatic :—" I reject altogether the idea
of recording standard measures by hiding them with the utmost
ingenuity."

Sir Henry James, the Director of the Ordnance Survey, and
supposed to understand measurement, objects to the unscientific
way Mr. Smyth has conducted his calculations, by first assuming
a theory, and then dragging in figures to accommodate it.   He
complains that his averages have been incorrectly made.   The
Professor has certainly acknowledged certain errors.   While
Vyse made 9168, why did he take 9142 for his base ? especially
after Mr. Inglis of Glasgow had, for the first time, laid bare the
four corner sockets, getting 9120, 9114, 9102, and 9102.   Sir
H. James, accepting 9168, finds the 360 Derahs, or Egyptian
land cubits, go into it 25·488 times ; therefore he concludes that
" the measures for the base of the Great Pyramid were set out
on the ground with the *Derah* or cubit of 25·488 inches.   This

differs from Mr. Taylor's 25·025, and Sir Isaac Newton's 20·699.

As to the exact relation between this cubit—changed at times by the professor himself—and the earth's axis, it is rather curious that while the professor took the polar measure, and Mr. Taylor that for lat. 30°, both gentlemen agree in their round numbers.

Sir James T. Simpson is sharp upon the professor, styling his theory fit " only for old women and womanish men." He makes merry about the number *five*. As to the polar axis story, he shows his calculation of a page of Mr. Smyth's book, which is just one eighty-millionth part of the polar axis, &c. But banter is not argument; neither is there logic in the funny but hardly proper way in which he thus refers to the coffer :—

" In short, to use the words of Prof. Smyth, ' that wonder within a wonder of the Great Pyramid, viz., the porphyry coffer,' —that ' chief mystery and boon to the human race which the Great Pyramid was able to enshrine,'—' this vessel of exquisite meaning,' and of ' far-reaching characteristics,'—mathematically formed under alleged Divine inspiration as a measure of capacity (and, according to M. Jomard, probably of length also) for all men and all nations, for all time,—and particularly for these latter profane days,—is, in simple truth, nothing more and nothing less than an old and somewhat misshapen stone coffin." Sir James was neither a mathematician nor a poet.

Still, he has some reason to say, "The coffer, though an alleged actual standard of capacity measure, has yet been found difficult or impossible to measure." After the professor's quoting 25 for a measure, he finishes by adding another of his own. In 1864 he had the capacity 70,970 English, or 70,900 pyramid

inches.   In 1867 he advanced to 71,250.   Mr. Taylor had
71,328, the cube of the cubit of Karnac.

While, however, Sir Edmund Beckett shows the inconsistency
and inapplicability of Mr. Smyth's 25 inch cubit standard, he
admits the teaching qualities of the sarcophagus, though believing it indicated *another* cubit.   "At the same time," says he,
"the pyramid and the famous marble coffer in the King's
Chamber (which was doubtless, also, Cheops' coffin, until his
body was "resurectionised" by the thieves who first broke into
the pyramid) do contain clear indications of having been
designed in very careful proportions, and by means of another
' rule,' or cubit, of which definite multiples appear everywhere,
unlike Mr. Smyth's imaginary cubit, nowhere, with an astronomical indication of its date, which satisfied no less an astronomer
than Sir John Herschel."

The mystical philosopher, the Chevalier de B., wrathfully
exclaims, " And so the huge sarcophagus of the mighty temple
of Cheops, in which Initiates were designed to be typically born
again of water and of the spirit, becomes a corn-measurer in the
eyes of the great British mathematicians."   Dr. Birch, our chief
Egyptologist, is quite opposed to the standard measure argument.

M. Dufeu views the professor's theory as very imaginary, and
adds, " Each of these authors, pre-occupied with his own system,
has rejected all those of his predecessors in order to give advan-
tage to his own."   Yet he, too, has his theory, and his cubit too.
" The sarcophagus," says M. Dufeu, " was the *standard of the
national measures* of Egypt; that is to say, of the Nilometric
cubit."   The latter is nearly $20\frac{2}{3}$ inches.

He thus lays it down :—" We have combined together the

three exterior dimensions and the three interior, and we have arrived at a result very certainly as unforeseen as unhoped for; that is to say, to discover in that double and marvellous combination of exterior and interior dimensions of the monolith together, the *standard of the Nilometric* cubit of 360 noctas."

By his system of calculation he reduces everything to noctas. A cubit is divided into six palms; the palm into four dactyles; and the dactyle into fifteen noctas. There are thus 360 noctas to the cubit, or about $17\frac{11}{26}$ to an inch. He proceeds on the system of *tens*. Thus he multiplies the box length, 7·3027 feet by 100, making 730·27 feet for the base. That he takes as a stadium, 500 to a degree of earth's surface.

He distinctly says that "almost all the monuments of Egypt are material, and consequently destined to preserve some ancient measure." This is perfectly true, as could easily be proved, and is another indication that the pyramid was not intended as the one standard of measure, though marking what was a standard at the time.

His Nilometric cubit is what Sir Edmund Beckett points out in the mean of 20·73 inches, though the coffer to him is "no exact multiple of a cubit in any of its dimensions." He deems it contained the measure of "the cube of a double cubit of about 41·46." The half of that is the cubit of 20·73 inches. The double Karnac cubit, he says, was between 41·398 and 41·472. That is assumed by Mr. Taylor a Jewish measure, while Ezra's cubit, he believes, is the royal or Memphis cubit. The measures of 2 Chron. iii. 3 are different from the thirty cubits of 1 Kings vi. 2; he supposes those thirty equal to the 120 others.

The variety of cubits is very confusing. M. Jomard gives in metres the following :—cubit of Megyas, or Nilometer of Rhoda

Island, 0·5385 ; Pykbelady, or country cubit, 0·5773 ; Black cubit of Caliph, 0·5196 ; Royal Arab, 0·6157; Roman, 0·4434; Hebrew, 0·5541 ; Nilometer, or New Greek, 0·5390 ; Constantinople, or Cairo, 0·674 ; Elephanta, 0·527 ; Royal Babylonian, 0·5131 ; cubit of Herodotus, Samos, Moses, Ezekiel, Babylon, &c., 0·4618, or 17 inches. Sir Gardner Wilkinson refers to cubits from 24 to 32 digits. The Talmudists had a cubit for the proportions of the human body, 25·61 ; but, to the steps of the inner court, 24·74. The supposed secret cubit was 24·91. The Harris cubit of Thebes is 20·65 inches. Perring's cubit of the pyramid is 20·628 inches. Wilkinson gives one at 20·5786. The Babylonian, afterwards Jewish, has been rated at 20·886 and 20·676. In the British Museum may be seen the double cubit of Karnac, found enclosed between two stones. Though 3250 years old, the wood is not decayed. The length is 41·46 inches. Mr. Taylor declares that the cube root of the contents of the sarcophagus will give the length of the Karnac cubit. The shorter Greek cubit was only 18·24 inches. The Memphis cubit, recently found, is said by Drovetti to be 522 millemetres, or an eighth more than the ancient cubit. Jomard is of opinion that the ancient Egyptian was twice lengthened in ancient times 3 digits, and by a palm or 4 digits in modern times. Sir H. James found the Derah still in use as the cubit of Egypt, being 25·488 inches. Roubiliac Couder, on *Ancient Metrology*, declares that Fergusson's statement of the Jewish cubits being respectively 15, 18, and 21 inches, is contrary to Scripture.

There is a similar difficulty about the stadium. The Olympium is put at 606·9 feet. Mr. Wilson has a stadium of 281 feet from 600 Greek feet. But Mr. Fergusson says, "The Eng-

lish is to the Greek or Egyptian foot as 75 is to 76 exactly."
He thinks, though Herodotus gave the base at 800 feet, that
"the side of the pyramid was intended to be an even number of
500 cubits." Jomard has the Egyptian foot to be 11 inches, 4
lines, 46 parts. A thousand Egyptian feet would make ten plethra.
Wilson makes the Grecian foot 12·0875 inches. The stadium is
calculated at 100 orgyia, one of which was supposed to be the
space between outstretched hands, or 6 feet. Greaves rates the
great stadium at 700 feet. The Egyptian stadium is said to be
327·27 feet. Herodotus calls the side 8 plethra; a plethron is a
sixth of a stadium. There are measures evidently of 500 and
600 stadia to a degree, though Jomard regards the last as
applicable to the oblique height of the pyramid.

Prof. Smyth, while highly extolling the pyramid cubit as of
Divine inspiration, is very severe upon the French metric system.
He condemns it on philosophical grounds, as it is based upon the
proportion to a quadrant of the earth's surface, which is not so
true, as he supposes, as the pyramidal, on the semi-axis principle.
But he more strongly condemns it as *infidel*, because it was
established in 1796, when the French were said, most absurdly
and erroneously, to have been a nation of atheists, inasmuch as
they objected to the rule of priests and kings. The French
metre is 39·37 inches. Mr. Petrie compares the more simple
pyramidal measure of one ten-millionth of the earth's radius
with the French standard of a ten-millionth of a curved terrestrial quadrant. The standard of weight is dependent on that of
measure. Prof. Smyth found that a pyramid pint weighed a
pound at 68°; and that 5 pyramid cubic inches weighed a pound.

Many thoughtful persons are ready to acknowledge that in

the pyramid a standard of weights and measures can be identified, though a difference of opinion may exist as to the relative amount; but they are unable to see that the pyramid was constructed with the express view of maintaining and of exhibiting that standard.

Attention must now be drawn to the supposed direct astronomical teaching of the pyramid.

12. AN ASTRONOMICAL OBSERVATORY.

As the Tower of Babel was in olden times believed to have been erected for the purpose of observing the heavens, so have pyramids been thought to have been raised with a similar intention. The tops, it was said, would have been admirable platforms; while the long passages, pointing, as they all did, toward the pole, would have made admirable day-telescopes.

Norden, the Dane, two centuries ago, saw one fatal objection to the theory. He remarks, "The top of the Second Pyramid, still covered with granite marble, cut so smoothly that no one can ascend it, decides absolutely that the pyramids were *not* built to serve as observatories." Volney, too, was shrewd enough to detect another objection; saying, "because it could not have been necessary to erect *eleven* observatories so near each other as the eleven pyramids of different sizes which may be seen from Djiza."

Plato's suggestion must therefore be set aside. So clever a people as the Chaldean priests would be hardly likely to build a tower on the low *plain,* either for safety from another Deluge or for elevation towards the skies, when they had ranges of mountains bounding their valley promising so much better sites. As to the passages of the pyramids furnishing telescopic conveniences, that accommodation could not have lasted longer than the time necessary for the workmen to go in and out, when not only were the passages blocked up, but the very entrance was so well concealed that no tradition existed to point out the locality.

M. Jomard, when with Bonaparte in Egypt, could not help exclaiming, " It is very remarkable that the openings of pyramids are all to the north." The passage seemed fitted for an observatory, as "it formed a true tube," said he, "at the mouth of which it would be possible, I presume, to see the stars during the day." He was satisfied that "one could at the lower point see the circumpolar stars pass the meridian, and observe exactly the instant of that passage." But M. Dufeu remarked on the idea, " that could have been but a secondary destination."

Prof. Piazzi Smyth fears " that astronomers must dismiss that favourite and frequently-published notion of their own shop, from the desires of their hearts ; for," adds he, "seeing that the passage was closed immediately after the building of it by a large stone portcullis, raisable only with immense difficulty, and on some few special occasions, its opportunities for observation would certainly have been far too rare to satisfy the practical needs of a working observatory."

13. ITS OWN LATITUDE.

Mr. Wild, C. E., of Zurich, said that the pyramid proclaimed the latitude of the place.

First, he found the entrance was 30 cubits above the base. His cubit is the ordinary one, about $20\frac{1}{2}$ inches. This indicates the latitude 30° N. Then he takes the pyramidal isosceles triangular side, and sees in 30° half the angle of the apex of a true isosceles. Afterwards, he gets another 30° from Euclid, as it is half the central angle of a regular hexagon. The six angles meeting at the centre are equal to four right angles, or 360°; one sixth of that would be 60°, and the half, 30°. Regarding the hexagonal principle for the pyramid of Gizeh, he discovers the heptagonal for the temples of Thebes. The central angle of a heptagon is 51° 25′ 42″, and the half is 25° 42′ 51″. He places the latitude of Thebes at 25° 43′.

Prof. Smyth assures us that "the Great Pyramid is as happy in its unique situation as in its extraordinarily exact construction." At the angle of 26° 18′ for the passage, he requires for the observation of the Polar star 2170 B. C. the latitude of 30°; or rather, 29° 59′ 59·2″. Then he approximately obtains the latitude another way. The angle of the north air-channel is, he says, 33° 42′, while that of the passage is 26° 18′; a mean between these numbers gives nearly 30°.

14. ITS OWN AGE.

In the astronomical argument, it is affirmed by Mr. Smyth and others that the fact that such a conjunction as the then Polar star and the Pleiades being seen, or to be seen, along the line of the passage, at the angle 26° 18′, 2170 B.C., proves the building or finishing of the pyramid to have been at that very date.

But other singular coincidences arise to support that era. The Rev. F. R. A. Glover, M.A., thus comments on the subject: "There is a mark of special providence within the pyramid, made 2170 B.C., which is responded to by a corresponding mark in a series of chronological passages, at the distance of 2170 inches, on a scale of an inch of space measuring a year of time;

which testifies, in a hard geometrical, irrefutable manner, in concurrence with *an* astronomical date, cosmically developed, to the fact, that at the time of the Advent in the year One of the Christian era, *was meant to be there*, and *thereby* indicated 2170 years before by the builder of the Great Pyramid, or whoever inspired the building of that work."

Mr. Casey, in *Philitis*, has a further description. After saying that the first Ascending Passage represents the Mosaic dispensation of 985 inches from the Dispersion to Moses, and 1542 thence to the Advent, he traces back 2170 inches to a little distance down inside of the slanting entrance passage, and shows the rectangular joints of the great stones forming the sloping walls are made nearly vertical in two successive instances only. "Then," says he, "the two strikingly visible separations of continuity in the walls are followed by a thin, fine, but exquisitely true line, ruled at six inches behind the last of these separations, and in that line is contained the position answering to 2170 B.C."

The mark was a line ruled on the stone from top to bottom of the passage wall at right angles to its floor. But what was wanted was "the distance from the nearest joint to the drawn line." This was ascertained to be $2170\frac{1}{2}$ one side, and $2170\frac{2}{5}$ on the other, in pyramid inches. "This testimony," adds Mr. Casey, "satisfies me, and fills me with thankfulness and joy."

But M. Dufeu has another calculation, founded on a new set of historico-mathematical principles, connected with the lists of kings by Manetho, by which he concludes that the pyramid was built at the beginning of the Sothic period. He finds the height of the hypogeum, he says, from the soil of the syringe to the roof to be 2920 noctas—two Sothic periods of 1460 years. As one Sothic age was 1322 B.C., the addition of 2920 would give 4242 B.C.

His analysis of Manetho's list, and its identification with chronology, would be out of place here. But he draws thence a conclusion, to be read in his *Quatre Pyramides de Gizeh*, that the 202 steps of the pyramid indicate the age of the building, as the number is referable to the so-called chronological height of the royal builder. The height of the pyramid he calls 262 cubits. From this he substracts 60 for the age of Menes, the first king, and gets 202.

The height of the King's Chamber he discovers to be one-fifth of the chronological height of the builder in the lists:— "demonstrating that the pyramid had been erected 808 years after the rise of Menes, first king, founder of the Egyptian dynasties, and, consequently, by the Cheops of Herodotus, Kufu of the Monuments, Souphis of Manetho, whose elevation was precisely placed, after the royal lists of this chronographic priest, 808 years after that of Menes." This would bring it to the time indicated by Rougé and Mariette Bey, over 4000 B.C.

Dufeu declares there is "perfect accord existing between the indications of the lists of Manetho and the length of the syringe of the hypogeum, the number of the steps, and the vertical height of the Great Pyramid, the height of its chambers, called the King's or the sarcophagus, and the heights of the chambers called Sepulchral of the three other pyramids."

The overwhelming difficulties in the way of the reception of 2170 B.C., and the historical agreements with 4242 B.C., will incline many readers to prefer M. Dufeu's coincidences to the coincidences relied on by Mr. Smyth.

15. THE CIRCUMFERENCE OF THE EARTH.

"The Pyramid of Cheops," writes the author of *The Solar System of the Ancients*, "may be regarded as a teocalli, or terraced pyramid, having the contents equal one half the circumference of the earth." By a reduction to *units*, he shows that five cubes of ten times the inclined side would produce the amount of the diameter of our orbit.

"The Pyramid of Cheops," he says again, "might be called the Pyramid of the Sun, as it denotes the time of descent from the earth to the sun. The number of steps accord with the number of half diameters of the sun, which equal the half diameter of the earth's orbit, and the pyramid itself equals the half circumference of the earth." He adds, "Possibly the race that constructed the pyramid might have found a difficulty in agreeing as to the comparative diameters of the earth, sun, and orbit of the earth, and so left the pyramid truncated or incomplete."

Of course, 360 times the length of a degree will give the circumference of the earth. "But," says Dufeu, "the length of the side or base of the Great Pyramid represented the stadium of 500 to the degree, and, consequently, the degree of the great circle." At 600 stadia to the degree he obtains the slant height of the pyramid. Thus, a degree, according to Jomard, is 110,827·68 metres. A six-hundredth part of that is 184·712 metres; but the slant height, being 184·722 metres, is very close to it.

Mr. Gliddon was no mystic in 1843, when he said, "Whether the Great Pyramid be 454 feet high, or 474, is to us a matter of indifference." To us more modern readers it matters a good deal. M. Dufeu attached importance to the height. He once wrote how, by the reckoning of 500 to a degree, " we have been able to discover the geodesic marks of the monument, and determine even, in suspecting it, the height given to its apex, or imaginary geometrical summit, or to the half-column (cippe) placed upon the platform crowning the pyramid, in order to give to this the vertical and mathematical height necessary that it might be a precious geodesic standard."

It is in this vertical height that he gets the standard of the measure of the earth.

Mr. John Taylor finds the height of the pyramid to be $\frac{1}{270,000}$ of the earth's circumference. Dividing 270,299 by 3·14157, and multiplying the result by the height of the pyramid in pyramid inches, 5825, he obtains 500,176,400 inches. Now, according to Piazzi Smyth, " the equatorial axis of the earth " is " somewhere between 502,000,000, and 503,000,000." The Edinburgh astronomer gets a mean result of 500,490,700 from the pyramid's measure; and he assumes the polar axis at 500,495,000 inches.

Mr. Taylor says that a band encircling the earth of the breadth of the base of the Great Pyramid will contain 100,000,000,000 square feet. Taking a twelfth of the length in pyramid inches, 762·5, and multiplying by 3·14159, he divides the result with 100,000,000,000, and realises 500,946,700 inches.

" It is probable," he thinks, " that a deeply-incised line was carved at the commencement, representing, in the first instance, the length of five royal spans, or 51,840 English inches, as the standard for the measure of the diameter; and in the second, the length of 150 pyramid inches, or 163,635 English inches, as the standard for the measure of the circumference."

Referring to 1600 talents for onions, &c., in Herodotus, the mystical Mr. Taylor says, "In the case of the circumference of the *present* earth, as also in the diameter of the *former* earth, the figures which Herodotus saw, and which the interpreter made vocal to him, were those which, when applied to a well-known measure of space with which the founders of the pyramid were familiar, will exactly express both of these numbers, amounting to the numerical power of the Arabian figures ; amounting, in the former instance, to 48,000,000 royal spans, or 497,664,000 English inches ; and the latter, to 1,440,000,000 pyramid inches, or 1,570,896,000 English inches."

Believing in the universal and destructive Deluge, and an earth changed by that Deluge in size, he says, "The founders would naturally desire to preserve a memorial of that earth which had been destroyed, that it might be compared with the new earth, from which they perceived it to differ."

On the other hand, we have Dufeu coming to a somewhat similar result on the assumption that the pyramid indicates 500 measures to the degree. Upon his system of tenths, he multiplies by 100 the length of the sarcophagus. This brings 730·27 feet. Multiplying by 500, he gets 365,134·5036 as the measure of a degree. That multiplied by 360 gives 131,448,421·2960 as the equatorial circumference of the globe ; Laplace stating that as 131,456,276·4778 shows the pyramid correct within 7854 feet. Some, again, take 100 times the coffer—730·27 feet, and multiply by 180,000 stadia to realise 131,448,421·296.

A French writer remarks that "it is not by chance that the Egyptian foot equals 360,000 to a degree." He considers that "it is thus certain that these measures have been drawn from the dimensions of the earth, and that they are derived from them, following the sexagesimal progression." Dufeu sees "in the vertical height of the Great Pyramid the standard of two of the great itinerary measures of the earth."

16. THE TRUE SHAPE OF THE EARTH.

We moderns are aware that this home of ours is not a regular globe, seeing that it is an oblate spheroid, with a bulging out at the equator, or flattening at the poles.

Hekekyan Bey, who is so full of the wonders of the pyramid as to say, "This Siriadic monument masonifies information which would fill volumes," has seen how it can express this polarity difference.

"The square root," he writes, "of the three-fifths of the difference between the length of the side of the rock platform, and twice the measure deducted from it to obtain the length of a side of the first course of masonry on the platform, gives the measure of the proportion of the polar compression to the equatorial diameter."

These he finds to be 302·2 to 301·2. In this way he gets the equatorial axis 8,752,847,053·3 noctas, and the polar 8,723,890,885·9.

Dufeu, in his system of calculation, obtains for the imaginary height of the pyramid 692·0937. This, says he, is one-hundredth part of the flattening of the earth at the pole, or one two-hundredth of the difference of the diameter at the equator and the axis of rotation. Though Laplace declares for 68,671·123, yet the mean of modern measures for this flattening is 69,209·8708. But it will be seen that the pyramid measure very nearly approaches the last as 100 × 692·0987 produces 69,209·87.

This height is thus obtained. He does not believe the pyramid ever higher than the present platform of 202 steps, or 450 feet 10 inches. He supposes a *cippe*, pole, or column of 6·827 metres to represent the imaginary apex. Thus he concludes the elevation above the lowest level of the Red Sea to be 692·1785 feet. M. Jomard originally suggested the *cippe* top. The platform base is now about 150 feet above the level of the desert.

17. THE DENSITY OF THE EARTH.

Citing a passage in Isaiah, upon " weighing the mountains in scales," Mr. Piazzi Smyth thinks he detects the *mean density of the earth* " to have been introduced into the capacity and weight measures of the pyramid at a time when it was an utter impossibility to men ;" that is, he supposes it pleased the Most High to *reveal* what astronomers have only recently discovered by science.

He finds the coffer contents to be 70,970·2 inches, and the coffer weight of water at 68° to be 17,905·500 gallons. Thence he gets by a division of these two quantities the approximate density of 5·672.

Mr. William Petrie has ascertained that the mass of the pyramid is to the earth as 1 to $10^{5 \times 3}$. He estimates the weight of the pyramid at 5,273,834 pyramid tons, and that of the earth 5,271,900,000,000,000,000,000. Reckoning the mean density of the earth at 5·7 times water, he regards the earth as exactly a thousand billions times the weight of the pyramid.

Mr. St. John Day, after noting that the exterior dimensions

of the sarcophagus or coffer are twice those of the interior, proceeds to demonstrate that, taking the internal cubical measurement at 71,250 inches, if we divide 71,250 by the recognised
mean density of the earth, 5·7, we obtain in the result, 12,500,
the weight of the coffer of water at the temperature of 68°. He
realises the coffer contents, 71,250, by multiplying the cube of
50 pyramid inches by the density, 5·7, and dividing the whole
by 10. The weight of the pyramid is declared to be $\frac{1}{10}$ 5 × 3 of
the weight of the globe.

Sir Edmund Beckett ridicules the attempt to make the
pyramid tell this density tale, especially as its advocates have
"the figures wrong, according to all the received measures, from
Newton's to the present day."

18. THE DISTANCE OF THE SUN.

A very simple law has been found for this calculation. It is
to multiply the height of the pyramid by the ninth power of the
number 10.

The steps of the building establish the relation of ten and
nine; so much so, that it was thought two poles, of 10 and 9
feet respectively, were set up at right angles, for guidance to the
workmen.

As the height bears a definite relation to the base, the one as
radius, the other as circumference, the accurate measurement
of the base will give the proper ideal height. Mr. Piazzi
Smyth makes the latter 5819 inches of our own times. But Mr.
Wm. Petrie estimates 5835 as nearer the truth.

The distance of the sun, by the ninth power of 10 multiplied
by 5819, will be about 91,840,000 miles; but by 5835 inch-

height, 92,093,000. Currently, the distance has been reckoned 95,000,000. More recent calculations have placed it some three millions less. The pyramid measurement, therefore, is more correct according to modern data.

The sun's distance is estimated at one thousand million times the height of the pyramid.

19. THE DAYS IN A YEAR.

Some curious calculations are brought out by Prof. Smyth, Captain Tracey, Mr. Petrie, Mr. Yeates, and others, upon the number of days in the year.

Mr. Thomas Yeates, in 1833, started the view, " whether or not the Great Pyramid of Ghizeeh was designed as a monument of the discovery of the Egyptian year." Again, he says, " The measure of the pyramid will be found to agree with the number of days in the solar year. Moreover, admitting my exposition of the ark of Israel to be correct, then will its measures of length and breadth be found to correspond in cubits with the number of days in the lunar year, viz., 354."

As mentioned elsewhere, Mr. Yeates identified the pyramid with Noah's ark. " The form of the ark," he said, " was quadrangular, and consisted of four equal sides, or parallelograms, of which the measure of one is given in three numbers—300, 50, and 30 cubits." Again, " The four sides include four rectangular parts of one dimension in length and breadth; and the whole equal a square of 350 cubits, inside measure, and four more for the outside, making in all 354 cubits, or about 737½ feet (25 inches to a cubit). Compare this with the measure of the Great Pyramid."

Mr. Wm. Petrie shows that the side of the pyramid will equal 365·3 multiplied by the cubit of 25·025 British inches. Assuming the ancient vertical height as 5813 inches, he would multiply that sum by the ninth power of 10, to realise the radius vector. He finds the number of days to go a round number of times into the circumference of the earth's orbit. The latter is taken at 36,525,430,000,000; and the former, 365·25636. But that circumference is associated with the perpendicular 5813; being thus produced—$5813 \times 10^9 \times$ twice $3\cdot1416 = 36,528,430,000,000$.

Prof. Hamilton L. Smith of New York, according to Mr. Piazza Smyth, taking "one length and two breadths of the King's Chamber for radius in a trigonometrical computation with the peculiar passage angle 26° 18′ 10″, the resulting sine, or length of the vertical side of the triangle, where the above radius is hypotheneuse, brings out exactly the year-day number, 365·242, &c." He also shows that the height of the niche in the Queen's Chamber, taken as 182·62, multiplied by 2 will give 365·24 solar days. He finds this height of the niche, if taken as 185 multiplied by 3·1416, and then by 10, will bring 5812, the height of the pyramid; but taken as 182·62, multiplied by 10 and divided by 2, the base, 9131, is obtained.

Capt. Tracey, R. N., has some pretty mathematical results from the Ante-chamber to the King's Chamber. The length of 116·26 inches he notes to be partly of granite, partly of limestone. The granite portion is 103·033 in pyramid inches, which are about a thousandth part larger than the British. Taking 103 for the side of a square, he gets the area of a circle whose diameter is 116·26. This amount multiplied by 3·14159, the proportion of circumference and diameter, brings out the days 365·24.

The King's Chamber is 412·132 pyramid inches long. With that as a diameter, the circle would equal a square whose side was 365·242 ; and this, in sacred cubits, is the length of the socket side of the pyramid.

Professor Smyth takes the 26 holes in the ramps of the gallery for days, and the 14 roof over-lappings for months, to get 364 days to the year. He then leads us to the Ante-chamber and the four grooves, one of which only holds the portcullis. Excepting, therefore, one year in four, we have to add but one day to 364 ; in leap year, two days must be added. He observes, too, that the groove filled by the portcullis is of less width than the other grooves ; and so concludes that less than one day in four must be added, as the year is not quite 365¼ days in length.

Another curious coincidence is pointed out by him. There is a great step by the upper end of the gallery, which is 90½ inches. That, says he, " which increased for the ruling angle of the place, goes close to 366 times into the circumference of the pyramid, eminently reminding, therefore, of the days contained in a year."

But Mr. Petrie discovered that the base of the pyramid divided by 365·242 would equal the *ten-millionth part of the earth's radius*. Sir Henry James got the base 764 from 360 derahs, or cubits, of 25·488 inches for days. Mr. Wild, C. E., determines that the relation of the Second and Third Pyramids brings out similar results.

20. THE LAW OF GRAVITATION.

The author of the *Solar System of the Ancients*, informs us that " the pyramid, like the obelisk, still points to the heavens as an enduring record of the laws of gravitation, though it has ceased to be intelligible for countless ages." He remarks, in another place, " The Pyramid represents the variation of the time, and the pagoda the variation of the velocity."

As the Great Pyramid is the present subject of enquiry, the obelisk teaching must be deferred for another publication. It will then be satisfactorily seen that the obelisk is one of the most perfect mathematical puzzles ever constructed. It stands the test of modern scale of descent by gravitating force, and elucidates the principle exactly. It is a masonified lecture on conic sections. It illustrates the fact that the most recondite theories of geometry and natural science were practically made use of in Egypt 5000 or 6000 years ago.

The pyramid, not less than the obelisk, which it resembles, can thus answer the enigma of gravitation, generally *supposed* to have been *discovered* by Sir Isaac Newton through the accident of an apple falling from a tree.

21. TIME OF DESCENT TO THE MOON AND SUN.

The number of steps to the pyramid, calculated at 219, has served Mr. Wilson with another curious astronomical coincidence, or teaching.

"The Pyramid of Cheops," says he, "will represent the time of descent from the earth to the moon through 219 semi-diameters of the moon, as well as the time of descent from the earth to the sun, through 219 semi-diameters of the sun. The bases of the pyramids will in both cases be in the centre or orbit of the earth ; but, in the descent to the sun, the apex of the external pyramid will be in the centre of the sun, and in the descent to the moon the apex of the external pyramid will be in the centre of the moon. The axis of the external pyramid is supposed to be divided into 219 equal parts, or 219 semi-diameters."

Again, he writes,—" We suppose the Pyramid of Cheops might have been dedicated to the sun, because it represented the semi-diameter of the sun and the semi-diameter of the earth's orbit, as well as the time of descent from the earth to the sun ; but now it appears that this pyramid will also represent the semi-diameter of the moon, and the semi-diameter of the earth's orbit, as well as the time of descent from the earth to the moon. So the Pyramid of Cheops might have been dedicated to both the sun and moon."

He also writes :—" The Pyramid of Cheops indicates the half-circumference of the earth and the half-diameter of the earth's orbit. Its towering summit may be supposed to reach the heavens, and the pyramid itself to represent the law at the time of a body gravitating from the earth to the sun. The solid hyperbolic temple of Shoemadoo of Pegu represents the *law of velocity* corresponding to this law of the time."

22. PLANETARY DISTANCES.

Mr. John Wilson also reads the distances of planets in the pyramids. His calculation is by what he calls *units ;* thus, the side of the pyramid, 760 feet, he calls 648 units ; and the height, 405 units. Each unit is about 14·074 inches.

The distance of the moon, he explains, will be thus obtained. Twenty times the cube of the side will be five times the distance of the moon. Of course, the amounts must be reduced into units. The cube of the side of the base (648^3) would give a quarter the moon's distance. Four times the cube of the pyramid, or the cubes of the four sides, gives the distance of the moon. Ten times sixty cubes, or 600 cubes of the pyramid, gives the distance of Mercury; that of Saturn will be twenty-five times as much, or 15,000 cubes. The cube of twice the side (1296^3) will be the diameter of the moon's orbit. Twenty-five cubes of the perimeter yields the distance of the earth from the sun; which is as many cubes of the side of the base as the side contains Babylonian feet. This is 1600, the number of talents Herodotus *says* he saw recorded outside.

The sarcophagus is, according to Mr. Wilson, very suggestive. Ten times the breadth raised to the ninth power gives the distance of Neptune; and the depth raised to the ninth power, the distance of Jupiter. Half the square of the length to the ninth power gives that of Mars. Five cubes of 300 multiplied by the length is the diameter of Mercury's orbit. Two cubes of 200 multiplied by the contents of the inside gives 280 times the distance of the moon, *i.e.* the distance of Venus.

The Grand Gallery he regards as of the hyperbolic order.

If these coincidences appear to be far-fetched, others are open to the same charge.

23. THE RISE OF A POLAR STAR.

Among the interesting discoveries in connection with the pyramid is that by looking through the passage to the northern heavens, 2170 B.C., an observer would there distinguish the *then* Polar star, *Alpha Draconis*, crossing the meridian *below* the Pole, and by *Pleiades* crossing it *above*.

Prof. Smyth thus puts the case :—"At that precise moment, when the Pole star, with the temporary distance of 3° 42′ from the pole, was crossing the meridian *below* the pole, at the same moment, or in that one year *alone* of all known years, the bright central star of the Pleiades cluster, separately symbolised in the Grand Gallery, was also on the meridian, but *above* the pole ; and not only near the equator, but on the very same meridian as Precession then assigned to the Equinox." He adds,—"The combination of all these several events, or phenomena, could only have occurred, according to the precessional calculations of modern astronomy, at or close to the year 2170 B.C."

All must admit this a singular coincidence, like that of the conjunction of planets at the birth of the Saviour. "But what of that?" the reader may ask. It is inferred that the Divine skill, which ordered the arrangements of the King's Chamber, dictated the angle of that passage by which, at the epoch of construction, such a remarkable astronomical occurrence could be observed.

Our own Polar star was then, by the Precession of the Equinoxes, far distant from the North Pole of the heavens, as *a* Draconis now is. The latter was at its nearest station 2800 B.C. Mr. Smyth admits that "there was a former epoch, viz., 3400 B.C., when the Polar star was also at that foundation distance of 3° 42′ from the pole, but with totally opposite accompaniments."

Sir John Herschel declared : "A passage may be said to have

directly pointed at a Draconis, at its inferior culmination, at which moment its altitude above the horizon of Gizeh (lat. 30°) would have been 27° 9'." But, as elsewhere named, a date was first given to the astronomer. The Rev. Dr. Nolan says : " At the request of Col. Vyse, Sir J. Herschel calculated the place of the star which was Polar at the time when, *according to the reduced chronology,* the pyramids were erected."

Mr. Gliddon, the distinguished American Egyptologist, has a version of the matter. He relates that the tables prepared by Vyse and Perring in 1838 were submitted to Sir John, who wrote as follows :—" No other astronomical relation can be drawn from the tables containing the angles and dimensions of the passages ; for, although they all point within five degrees of the Pole of the Heavens, they differ too much, and too irregularly, to admit of any conclusions." Again : " The exterior angles of the building are remarkably uniform ; but the angle 52° is not connected with any astronomical fact."

The American was very decided upon the astronomical question. In 1842 he denied the fact of pyramid observations. " First," says he, " by their extraordinary variety and number ; and secondly, in Ethiopia, by their fronts facing all points of the compass, from N.E. to S.E. Thirdly, in Egypt, from the measurements made in 1839 by Mr. Perring, which demonstrate that the inclinations of the passages, as well as the relative position of each pyramid, vary so as to destroy all conformity to mathematical or astronomical purposes. These proofs against their astronomical utility are independent of the voluminous evidence to be gleaned from history, and from a glance at the monuments themselves, their localities and associations, which declare their sepulchral origin. *If*, as Sir John Herschel observes, the inclined passage into the largest pyramid of Gheezeh was made at an angle to correspond to *a* Draconis, this pyramid must have been built about the year 2123 B.C., which alone would suffice to upset Usher's epoch of the Deluge, 2348 B.C."

Some think the professor too dogmatic in his assertion about angles and dates. Why, it is asked, does he select 26° 18′ for the passage, which others state to be 26° 41′? Why should he light upon 2170 B.C. when others give no such precise date? When Col. Vyse, by actual measurement, made an angle 51° 50′ 51·52″, Mr. Taylor, to suit his theory, preferred to adopt 51° 51′ 14·3″, and Mr. Smyth another angle.

Mr. Agnew, in 1838, gave mathematical reasons for the angle being different. "The real angle of the dip," he writes, "or the angle *intended to be given* to it, was 26° 33′ 54″, being the inclination of a line from the middle of one side to the opposite corner, or the angle formed by the hypothenuse of a right-angled triangle with the greater of the two sides containing the right angle, these latter being to each other as 2 to 1." He thinks that "other passages with the same inclination may probably exist, leading in a zigzag direction to upper rooms on the levels of the other inscribed squares of the figure."

Sixty years ago Dr. Richardson said, "The supposition that this passage was intended as an astronomical instrument for measuring side-real time is scarcely tenable. Pyramids are prodigiously expensive and unmanageable machines; and the passage being so carefully sealed at the entrance precluded all possibility of using it as such. Besides, there being so many pyramids, all of them with passages looking to the north, and descending nearly with the same angle of inclination, they were probably intended to answer some other purpose than that of looking at the Polar star."

Mr. Fergusson the architect lays it down that "all these theories have failed, for a variety of reasons it is needless now to discuss ; but, among others, it may be mentioned that the angles are not the same in any two pyramids, though erected within a few years of one another, and in the twenty that were measured by Col. Vyse they vary from 22° 35′ to 34° 5′. The angle of the inclination of the pyramid to the horizon is more constant, varying only from 51° 10′ to 52° 32′, and in the Gizeh pyramids it would appear that the angle of the passage was intended to have been about one half of this."

Our own Nestor of Egyptologists, Dr. Birch, has this statement :—"It has been supposed that they were built to record an arc of the meridian, the earth's diameter, the revealed unit of measure, the *exact rise of the old Polar star, a Draconis*, and other points of cosmic or mathematical knowledge. These ideas do not appear to have entered into the minds of the constructors of the pyramids, who employed measures for their symmetrical construction."

In a letter the writer received from a distinguished scientist and official astronomer are these words :—"Astronomers do not as a rule agree with Piazzi Smyth's *deductions and conclusions*. His matters of fact are of course not disputed, and many of his discoveries are, I think, rather looked upon as curious and interesting coincidences, than as establishing his theories."

24. THE EQUINOXES.

It is an old classical notion that the pyramid, at certain times, never throws a shadow. There was a pretty general impression that it was erected as a true chronometer by marking solar changes. Plato, in this sense, called it the *dial*. Other contrivances were known that indicated these astronomical effects. The well at Syene reflected in its waters the image of the sun at the summer solstice. The equinoctial and solstitial points were in the very early times correctly observed.

The pyramid on the north side was in shadow from the autumnal to the vernal equinox, but light from the vernal to the autumnal at midday. It, therefore, followed that those who stood at the centre of the north base, at the equinox, would see the sun resting on the apex of the pyramid.

The orientation of the pyramid being so nearly perfect, having for its error, says Sir Edmund Beckett, but 5′, or one foot in its base line of 761, enables the structure to act as a gnomon. I may have been more exact once, there being some evidence of a twist, as from an earthquake. M. Defvignoles remarks that this orientation " could have served for the Egyptians to determine the time of the equinoxes, when the sun begins to enlighten the northern face, or when he ceased to shine there." This would only occur when the years of equinoxes suited the sun's rising.

Mr. Stewart, of America, has some observations :—" It follows from these dimensions, and the latitude under which this pyramid is erected, that fourteen days *before* the spring equinox, the precise period at which the Persians celebrated the revival of nature, the sun would cease to cast a shade at midday, and could not again cast it until fourteen days *after* the autumnal equinox. Then the day, or the sun, would be found in the parallel or circle of southern declension, which answers to 5° 15′; this would happen twice a year—once before the spring, and once after the fall, equinox. The sun would then appear exactly at midday upon the summit of this pyramid."

25. PRECESSION OF THE EQUINOXES.

The ancient year of the gods, 25,920 years, is one of many signs that Sir Isaac Newton's supposed discovery was known long before. Prof. Robinson says, "It is now very certain that the precession of the equinoxes was known to the astronomers of India many ages before Hipparchus. The Egyptians, also, had a knowledge of something equivalent to this, for they had discovered that the Dog-star was no longer the faithful fore-warner of the Nile, and they combined him with the star Fomal-haset in their mystical calendar."

The very fact of their having both solar and sidereal time would show a consciousness of moveable equinoxes.

Hekekyan Bey gives 50·34″ as the record of the annual recession, showing the excess of time over 365 days in the tropical and sidereal years. He takes 29° 57′ 30″ for the latitude.

But Mr. Casey, in the *Philitis*, a really valuable little pamphlet, points out that the pyramid itself declares the cycle of the precession, and that nearer to the modern acceptation than even the Asiatic great circle of 25,920 years. He declares that the two diagonals of the base of the pyramid, estimated in pyramid inches, measure 25,827. That number in years will be about the time the stars take to recover their several positions in relation to our pole.

Mr. Wild, C. E., nearly thirty years ago, had a pretty calculation of his own to prove the Great Pyramid a true chronometer, or time-measurer, and a dial in a higher sense than Plato meant when he applied that title to it.

As is well known, the entrance passage is not in the centre of the north side of the pyramid. Mr. Wild, who makes use of a cubit—the Memphis one—quite different to that employed by Prof. Smyth, assumes the eastern side from the entrance to be 210 cubits, and the western 238. The difference, 28 cubits, he discovers to be the exact distance, $0\cdot4758''$, indicated by Maedler as the annual diminution of the obliquity of the ecliptic.

As the entrance is 14 cubits eastward of the middle of the north face, he finds that "during the half of the year in which the sun lights the northern side of the pyramid (intended as a chronometer) the tropic retrogrades 14 cubits; that is, exactly the same distance as the entrance of the Great Pyramid is removed eastward from the middle of the northern face."

More singular,—" In 210 years the tropic retrogades 100", exactly in the same number of years as the eastern portion of the base contains cubits." That is, taking Maedler's rate of $0\cdot4758''$ for the year. " Then," says he, " in 500 years the tropic retrogrades 238"; that is, as many seconds as the western portion contains cubits."

Again,— " According to the above-mentioned operations, the proportion between the base and height of the pyramid is as 16 to 10. The tropic retrogrades in sixteen years the full length of the base, and in ten years the full height of the Great Pyramid; for the length of the base is $16 \times 28 = 448$ cubits, and the height is $10 \times 28 = 280$ cubits."

It is an equally remarkable coincidence that 25,000 times the annual diminution of 0·4758″, or 3° 18′ 15″, if added to what he recognises as the inclination of the entrance passage, 26° 41′, would give the latitude of the pyramid, 29° 59′ 15″. The difference between the inclination of 26° 41′ and that of the Ascending Passage, 26° 18′, is 23′. This amount represents 2900 years obliquity, or nearly one-ninth of the cycle of precession.

This very convenient pyramid gives astronomical results of as striking and as perfect a character for Mr. Wild with 20 inch cubits as for Prof. Smyth with 25 inch ones.

26. CONNECTION WITH SIRIUS, THE DOG-STAR.

Several writers, including Arabian philosophers, have fancied some "mystic correlation," to use the words of M. Dufeu, "between the design and age of the pyramid and the revolutions of Sirius, the judge-god of the dead."

In the present work the religious question can but be glanced at. Sirius was known as Sothis by the Egyptians, whence the so-called Sothic year, or revolution of 1460 years. Hermes, god of wisdom, says Champollion, was Sirius, or Sothis. Hermes is Thoth, or Anubis, the deity presiding over the dead, and yet being the originator of learning. Popular tradition among the Arabs, revived among certain mystical Christian writers of our own day, indicates Seth as the builder of the pyramid. Seth, in this case, is probably Sothis, or Sirius.

No star was so venerated in Egypt as Sirius, associated, as it was, with the time of the annual overflow of the Nile, which the rising of the star foreshadowed. The hieroglyphic for Sirius is, oddly enough, the triangular face of a pyramid. Dufeu and others suppose that the pyramid may have been dedicated to this venerated star or period. Proclus relates the belief in Alexandria that the pyramid was used for observations of Sirius.

Murtadi, 1584, says that the magical priest Saiouph made his abode, at the time of the Deluge, in the pyramid; "which," says he, "was a temple of the stars, where there was a figure of the sun, and one of the moon, both of which spoke." He mentions the great grandson of Noah, Bardesi, who, as priest, "applied himself to the worship of the stars." He adds, "It is reported that he made the great laws, built the pyramids, and set up for idols the figures of the stars."

M. Dufeu finds the total height from the soil of the syringe to the roof to be 2920 noctas, or twice the Sothic period of 1460 years. "We consider that," says he, "a proof that the Great Pyramid had been dedicated to this memorable Sothic period, or rather to Sothis, the star justly venerated in Egypt. One sees by that that the hypogeum takes its point of departure from the beginning of the revolution of Sothis anterior to the sixty years before the coming of Menes, the same as Manetho takes his point of departure from the initial point of that same revolution of Sothis, in attributing to Cerpheres a Sothic height of 839 years, or chronological noctas, at the moment when he founded the subterranean construction of the Great Pyramid."

Having come to the close of the interesting lessons of an astronomical kind, communicated by the Great Pyramid, we discover that the measurements are assumed to have some direct and important relation to religious subjects. Reference will therefore be made to some of these ideas.

27. THE UNITY OF GOD.

Prof. Smyth, in *Our Inheritance in the Great Pyramid*, thus writes: "The Great Pyramid, a pre-historic and entirely pre-Mosaic monument, had remained sealed in all its more important divisions, from the date of its foundation up to an advanced period of the Christian dispensation; and was then found, on being opened and examined, entirely free from that accursed thing which formed the leprosy of the East in ancient days—idolatry."

No hieroglyphics occur on the sarcophagus. This fact he declares to be "that astonishing isolation, not only from other pyramids, but from everything of Egyptian intentions, such as now appears to be, and to have been from the beginning, the attribute of the pyramids."

He contrasts it thus with the Sphinx; "That monster, an idol in itself, with a wig and painted cheeks, and symptoms typifying the lowest mental organisation, positively reeks with idolatry throughout its substance; for, when the fragments, or component masses, of its colossal stone beard were discovered in the sand-excavation of 1817, it was perceived that all its internally joining surfaces of the blocks had been figured, full of the 'impure' Egyptian gods."

It is unfortunate for the professor's theory that "impure" hieroglyphics were found in the pyramid, even the quarry marks of the two kings; and these, as in *all* cartouches of kings, are *idolatrous emblems*—the serpent and birds of Egyptian worship. In a subsequent work it will be shown that gods, and not *the* God, were the objects of adoration, even *before* the age of the pyramid.

28. DIVINE ORIGINATION OF MEASURE.

The assumption of some writers is, that a correct standard being of inestimable value, and it being faithfully exhibited by the pyramid, none could have originated such a scheme of weights and measures therein but Deity Himself.

There has been a time in the history of every race when nothing could occur beyond the comprehension of ignorance that was not attributed to the direct interposition of local divinities. In every language, perhaps, thunder is God's voice. An aerolite, or a lightning flash, was sent direct from the hand of the thunderer.

It was natural for the rude peasant Egyptians in the days of the pyramid to believe that their god Thoth had revealed a system of measures, a mode of building, or a style of writing, to their priests, but it is hardly according to modern habits of thought to see a necessity for Divine inspiration in such matters. Can there be more occasion for the Edinburgh professor to bring down the Deity for the regulation of the size of the sarcophagus in the pyramid, than for the President of the Royal Academy to require special inspiration from Jehovah for the earliest known, and yet most beautifully chiselled, sculpture of a pre-pyramid age?

It is the architect Fergusson who says, "It has been even asserted that God revealed to Cheops a variety of interesting astronomical information, and commanded him to build these facts into the Great Pyramid in British inches."

There is no mistake in the language of the advocates of inspiration. Prof. Piazzi Smyth says, "That metrology at large was a subject not beneath the dignity of Divine attention in the

earlier ages of the world, appears sufficiently (?) from the following commands issued by Divine revelation, in subsequent times,
to the particular people, in these words ; viz., " Thou shalt have
a perfect and just weight," &c.

Again he says, " Philitis, in the Greek of Herodotus, but
Melchisedek, as we believe, in Hebrew, controlled the Egyptian
king of the time to use the organised but peaceful bands of his
subjects in the erection of this prophetic building, whose *inspired design* they understood not." He gives his reason,
" touching the even earth immensurability of these measures
having been a problem entirely beyond the power of men either
of the pyramid day, or of any other day 4000 years therefrom—
unless they had received the aid of Divine inspiration from on high."

Elsewhere something may be said to show the high degree of
civilisation attained in pre-pyramid times, and the extreme probability that not only was the masonified pyramid-learning, so
admirably illustrated by Prof. Smyth, to a great degree lost very
soon after the death of Cheops, owing to disturbing invasions,
but that the knowledge of the arts suffered a most serious check.
In those ante-printing, and even ante-writing, epochs, it was
easy for certain kinds of intelligence to be absolutely and for
ever extinguished. The higher secrets of wisdom were confided
to but very few, and were never committed to letters.

Mr. John Taylor, the professor's teacher upon this religious
aspect of the pyramid, somewhat identifies Noah with the
building. He being the preacher of righteousness, " nothing
could more illustrate," he says, " this character of a preacher of
righteousness after the Flood than that he should be the first
to publish a system of weights and measures for the use of all
mankind, based upon the measure of the world."

29. INSPIRATION FOR CERTAIN TEACHING.

This, though a modern conception, is becoming a very popular one in certain circles of religious people. On that account it is to be treated with respectful attention. Pious convictions, and views supposed to be derived from, and sustained by, the Holy Scriptures, are not to be rejected with sneers, though judged ever so unreasonable. Some minds are more susceptible of the marvellous than others. Many believe they add to the glory of the Deity in the multiplication of instances of His direct interposition. There are those who style this *anthropomorphism,* and reject the pagan-like contrivance of bringing the Divinity too frequently and needlessly from the clouds.

Prof. Piazzi Smyth has been the most prominent advocate of the Divine origin and purpose of the Great Pyramid. In the present work only a glance can be given at his important theory. He finds, as he thinks, certain scientific truths of high interest, and some dearly-cherished religious dogmas, conveyed in the measurements and architecture of the building. He cannot conceive of this masonified intelligence otherwise than from God Himself. He calls it the "Temple of Inspiration;" and quotes 1 Chron. xxviii. 19, "The Lord made me understand in writing." He lays it down as a fixed principle, "If intention did really preside on the occasion, it could only have been the result of Divine inspiration imparted to certain men."

Mr. Fergusson, while admitting it as "the most perfect and gigantic specimen of masonry that the world has yet seen," seems to doubt the necessity of inspiration, saying, "There is no reason whatever to suppose that the progress of art in Egypt differed essentially from that elsewhere." There are those who see more beauty, finish, and skill in the Third Pyramid than the first. The Great Pyramid was clearly constructed upon the model of previously existing ones, though with some peculiarities of its own. One system of teaching runs through all the pyramidal structures, whether of Egypt, India, or America, pointing to one thought.

Prof. Hamilton Smith—like many who regard the ancients as fools—is so amazed at the scientific revelations of the pyramid, and, it may be added, pyramids, as to feel himself on the horns of a dilemma. He must either, he says, admit that in those long-past ages men knew as much as we do now, or that supernatural inspiration was granted to certain men, who were, whether they themselves understood the meaning of their own acts or not, to build an enormous edifice only to perpetuate this knowledge.

If it required the genius of some few men in the nineteenth century to reveal this thing—which is, however, doubted by the great mass of scientists now—of what practical use was the lesson at all? The pyramid was absolutely closed upon completion. The ignorant and the heathen were thus deprived of the benefit of this inspired teaching. And we, too, though believing in God, and understanding the astronomical lessons of the pyramid apart from its school, would have been still left in absolute ignorance of this mysterious and wonderful teaching upon religion and science had not a certain Mahometan ruler of Egypt, some thousand years ago, actuated by avarice, employed hundreds of men to force a way into the building.

After all, we may say with Sir James Simpson, " In relation to the Great Pyramid, as to other matters, we may be sure that

God does not teach by the medium of miracle anything that the unaided intellect of man can find out."

30. THE MEMORIAL OF THE DELUGE.

Prof. Smyth has pointed out that the passage, with its angle of 26° 18', looked toward the North Pole 2170 B.C., when the then Polar star was crossing the meridian. But, he observes that when that body crossed *below* the pole, the mouth of the Waterpot of Aquarius was crossing the meridian *above* the pole.

The event called the *Deluge*, always associated with Aquarius, and necessarily so, as the mystics affirm, is thus strongly fixed upon the Egyptian mind by such a constructive memorial of the passage of the constellation. Mr. Smyth, who recognises no mere celestial Deluge, and no partial terrestrial one; but an absolute and universal drowning of the whole globe, says that it "destroyed all pre-existing monuments." He evidently believes, like other mystics, that the Deluge had some mysterious connection with the ascendancy of Aquarius. He speaks of Aquarius being the "prominent constellation" at what he styles the "awful moment for man," when Draco was in the ascendant.

He is perfectly satisfied, by pyramid measurement, that the time of the Deluge would "be as surely very near 2800 B.C. as the date of the Great Pyramid building is close to 2170 B.C." In this estimate he adds 450 years to the commonly received Biblical chronology. He has as much right to give a date to the Deluge as the 300 known authorities had for their several 300 periods for that occurrence. If, too, his calculation

for the pyramid building be 2170 B.C., he must needs get a
great deal more time, between that date and the Deluge, than
what Usher and others afford him, in which to have enough
population, progress, and wealth for the construction of the
pyramid in Egypt.

31. THE SABBATH.

Those who contend for the antediluvian, or ante-Mosaic,
origin of the Divine institution of the Sabbath, suppose they
have confirmation of their opinion from the imagined Sabbatical
teaching of what some regard as a Divinely-inspired building.

The roof of the Gallery is seen to have *seven* overlappings—
a suggestive lesson.   The Queen's Chamber has *seven* sides ;
that is, the four walls, the floor, and the double roof.   Again,
the height of the Great Gallery is pronounced *seven* times that
of the ordinary passages.   At the angle of 26° 18′ the latter's
transverse height of 44·8 inches becomes 50 vertical, and this
is a seventh of 350, the vertical height of the Gallery.

" For what purpose," asks Mr. Piazzi Smyth, " is the Grand
Gallery holding up so notably to view seven of the said
standards ? "

The seven standards of length he would conclude to mean
standards of time.   The small passage represents the unit day,
and the Gallery is the week.   His conclusions are :—" That
violent and apparently unmeaning contrast of heights has the
noblest of reasons, viz., the typifying of the sacred division of
time ; and we see here, again, that in time, as well as in space,
the Great Pyramid embodies an idea which was entirely unknown to, or totally disobeyed by, the Egyptians."

The Sabbath idea of time was fully recognised, however, by Egyptians and Chaldeans.   The name of *Sunday* points to the fact, recognised by ancient Peruvians as well as ancient Egyptians. The number *seven* was, in Egypt, especially dedicated to Sirius, and was regarded as a sacred number.   In the chapter on the blocking of the Gallery, reasons are given by Mr. Agnew why the roof was lofty.   It is needless to point out to readers that the seven planets—the Sun, Moon, Mercury, Venus, Mars, Jupiter, and Saturn, objects of veneration in extreme antiquity —were associated with the division of time in weeks.   The very word *Sabbath* is said by Mr. George Smith to be of Assyrian origin.   But it is well for man, apart from Biblical sanction, that in Nineveh, Babylon, Egypt, and Peru, the necessity of one day's rest in seven was so distinctly laid down by the priest-hood.

32. MODEL FOR MOSAIC INSTITUTIONS.

Those who maintain, as one expresses it, that not "all the revelations of God to man have been transcribed into the Bible," and who declare that "the pyramid revelation is not a rival of the Bible but an impregnable out-work to defend the sacred citadel of Bible inspiration," see no difficulty in making Moses go to the pyramid for many things he afterwards incorporated into the Mosaic institutions.

Mr. Piazzi Smyth, among his many bold statements, has the following :—" Moses, having once received into his care the sacred cubit, took additional precautions for multiplying its copies and derivations, so successfully preserved by his country-men through fifty generations ; that sacred cubit being, in fact of length, as already proved, the unique smaller lineal standard of the Great Pyramid." But where did Mr. Smyth learn that Moses *received* the sacred cubit? and where is it taught that he multiplied its copies? Was not the pyramid closed long before his time, so that he could not get access to this standard?

Mr. Drach, F.R.A.S., asks, "Were the Mosaic tabernacle measures connected with the pyramid coffer as a metric standard?" He concludes they were so. He shows that the ark, mercy-seat, and burnt-offering altar were constructed after that scale.

But it is further assumed, that Aaron's rod was laid up in the ark as the standard cubit; that Solomon's laver was the same as the pyramid coffer; that the molten sea was a multiple of five; that the stone tablets of the ark were metric copies of the coffer, &c. One compares the two thus:—"The King's stone standard of the universal metric system deposited in the ark chamber of a Suphis pyramid." The ark itself was of that measure.

It is not wonderful that somebody else should still further mark the derivation of the Mosaic institutes from the Egyptians by saying, "The ark, also, contained an authentic copy of the hermetic books."

33. A MESSIANIC MONUMENT.

Although Mr. Piazzi Smyth and others had developed to so extraordinary an extent the religious aspects of the pyramid, and had affirmed so strongly that it was built by direct inspiration from the Most High, yet Mr. Casey, of Carlow, author of *Philitis*, wrote five years ago thus to his leader, Mr. Smyth: "Unless the Great Pyramid can be shown to be *Messianic*, as well as fraught with superhuman science and design, its sacred claim is a thing with no blood in it."

It is an old saying that the demand will provoke a supply. The desire for the Messianic procured from this very peculiar, and this every-theory-satisfying, pyramid some very conclusive Messianic token. Some writers assert that figures can be made to prove anything. But the lines of the pyramid are quite as accommodating. A miraculous origin being supposed, there were no difficulties in the multiplication of miracles. While the written Word was dark and obscure, the pyramid was light and clear. Isaiah, the glorious prophet, had but the dim sense of a coming One, though some commentators doubt whether he understood what he revealed. But the heathen builders of Egypt, ages before Moses and the Scriptures, knew all about it, and were able, by Divine counsel, to masonify even particulars of the life of Jesus in Palestine. (!!)

Coincidences are often remarkable, though not convincing. The story is told of the late Archbishop Whately, that one of his clergymen came to him in great exercise of mind about some novel application of the mystical number, 666. In the course of his enthusiastic appeal he observed His Grace, apparently indifferent to the harangue, scribbling on some paper. The curate rose hastily to say "Good day!" offended at this inattention. The old man quietly turned to him and said, "Mr. ———, I was listening to your remarks, and testing them by some calculations. You read such a person's name by the dreaded title of 666. I have been looking at your own name, and discover the alarming fact that it bears the number of the beast."

Captain Tracey published his *Pillar of Witness, a Scriptural View of the Great Pyramid*, dedicated to Mr. George Casey, and entering upon this theme.

The mysterious line in the Grand Gallery, measured off in pyramid inches, is made to tell some extraordinary things. But Mr. Menzies unfolds the Messianic mission of the pyramid in these words :—

" From the north beginning of the Great Gallery floor there, in southward procession, begin the years of the Saviour's earthly life, expressed at the rate of a pyramid inch to a year. Three-and-thirty inch years, therefore, bring us right over against the mouth of the well, the type of His death and His glorious resurrection too ; while the long, lofty Grand Gallery shows the dominating rule in the world of the blessed religion which He has established thereby, overspanned above by the thirty-six stones of His months of ministry on earth, and defined by the floor-length in inches as to its exact period."

A writer in *The Nation's Glory Leader*, a periodical devoted to millennial subjects, carries out the Messianic character of the pyramid, perhaps, beyond others of the same school. Coincidences help him to come to such conclusions. Speaking in the 53rd of Isaiah style respecting the pyramid, he says :—

" Its countenance is more marred than that of any other building, or remnant of a building, that, to my knowledge, is in existence. Assuming it to be true that the pyramid really is a Messianic structure, what a startling parallel is presented unto us ! ' His visage was so marred more than any man.' The side (*query* left side) of the huge structure being perforated by force ere the secret of the interior could be ascertained. The spear thrust into the side of Jesus by the soldiers is apparently a strict parallel as to what was essential to be done, in order that the secrets of eternity might become visible unto man. The outpouring of blood and water, which was necessary to complete the supplying of the means of gaining the secrets of eternity, appear all to have its parallel in the perforation of the pyramid by that down-rush of rubble which had been left in the Ascending Passage." (!)

With all due respect for the pious intentions of such Messianic interpreters, with their happy coincidences, some persons will suspect that the notion leans rather toward the *fancies* than the *facts* of the pyramid.

34. A TYPE OF CHRIST AND HIS CHURCH.

Among other *fancies* affording gratification to the pious mind of Mr. Piazzi Smyth is that the Great Pyramid typifies the union of the visible Church in the invisible Head.

He quotes Paul's words, Eph. ii. 19, "in whom all the building fitly framed together," as applicable to the case. All Christians were to be so united. But one thing was needed to complete the structure, and bind all in one indissoluble body. This was the corner-stone.

This five-sided, five-angled stone, for the top of the pyramid, he imagines must have been prepared a long while before the completion of the building; and, being often in the way of the workmen, who were then not more refined and scrupulous perhaps in their language than now, they abused it. In fact, it was the rock of offence. Yet this, which the builders despised, became the head stone of the corner, being thus a type of Christ, the rejected of men.

The prophetical character of the type is maintained in the rejoicings over the fixing of this stone, "while," as the professor puts it, " the Hycsos kings and royal brethren greeted the completion of this most peculiar and nobly-destined temple with the faultless cry of ' Grace, grace unto it ! ' "

35. THE SECOND COMING OF CHRIST AND THE MILLENNIUM.

To some persons it may seem strange that the pyramid should have been erected for such an object as to prophesy the millennium.   The discovery is certainly a very modern one.   The Rev. F. R. A. Glover declares it " a sign given 4040 years ago ; *first seen* in A.D. 1865 ; *first understood* in the autumn of 1872-73."

A clergyman describes the pyramid as " a link between the dispensation of Noah and the close of the fifth dispensation." " The use of it," says he, " is to be a sign and a witness unto the Lord of Hosts " of the cessation of the ages of oppression, of war, and injustice, in order to signalise and to aid the approach of the millennial dispensation."   He, with Prof. Smyth, sees in it the Hebrew prophet's " altar in the midst of Egypt, even a pillar in the border thereof, which shall be for a sign and a witness unto the Lord of Hosts in the midst of Egypt."

Undoubtedly the prophetical character of the pyramid is the most distinguished claim yet assumed for it, even in this age of the revival of symbolism, the era of Ritualism.   It is the marked and remarkable evidence of that strange yearning of modern life—sick of its materialism and of old dogmas—for idealising objects.   It is not mere sentimentalism, but something more profound and earnest in feeling.   Some think it a part of the revolt against creed, and the sign of a weariness of the authority of mere Scripture texts.   Others deem it a dissatisfaction with the demands of the Church, and a desire to find elsewhere a foundation and a guide.   Heaven and earth are being ransacked for something that will satisfy the soul.

As men have now become so clever as to acquire a knowledge of scientific facts, such as the size of the earth and its distance from the sun, facts revealed by God to the builders of the pyramid, and by them set to measure therein, Prof. Piazzi Smyth sees another of the signs of the approaching millennium. "May not these be symptoms," he asks, "that the stormy beginning of the first end is nigh at hand, the present dispensation nearly concluded, and a new one with more exalted ends and of a wider significance not far from commencing?"

This approaching fate of the world was once only to be read in the Book of Daniel; it is now to be learnt more distinctly from that marvellous tell-tale, the *Pyramid*.

M. Maillet, nearly 200 years ago, noted a crack or line, as if from an earthquake, the whole length of the Gallery. It is there where the mysteries have been just revealed.   Thus it is written:—"The Grand Gallery, the mightiest feature of the interior of the Great Pyramid, and the direct issue upwards and continuously of the Hebrew passage, *i. e.* of the separation of the Hebrews as a peculiar people to God, indicates the Christian dispensation and its history at the rate of, as before, a pyramid inch to a year, beginning at the north wall with the birth of Christ, and proceeding thence up the inclined floor of the Grand Gallery southward."

The professor thus finds, in 1542 inches, the date of the Exodus, 630 inches from the mark to indicate the date of the erection of the pyramid, 2170 B.C.   At 358 inches further he gets the Dispersion, and at 2790 B.C. the Deluge, though the last is placed in our Bibles at 2348 B.C.

From the north end, starting at the Dispersion, 2527 B.C., one may reach, says Mr. Casey, " the symbol of the bottomless pit, a chamber deep in the rock." But Mr. Smyth speaks of " where it begins on the north end with the date of the birth of the Saviour of mankind." Starting at that point, and going up the Gallery, he traverses about 156 feet or 1872 inches. But he calculates by Herschel's geometrical-cubit inch, which he styles the pyramid inch, which very slightly differs from our own, being one thousandth part longer, or 1·001 inch.

He gets to the upper or southern end of the Gallery, between the 1881 and 1882 inch marks. This he assumes to mark *the date of the millennium !*

" Here," he exclaims, " in all its solidity and overhanging imminence, is the southern wall, or practical termination of the Grand Gallery. Whatever, therefore, that feature symbolises terminates there too ; viz., in 1881-2 A.D." He is writing to the periodical, *Life from the Dead.*

In that date he gains the beginning of the end, the opening of the millennial age. But the full glories of that period are not to be experienced till fifty-three years after. The reason for that will appear. The reader is aware that a small, low passage leads from the Grand Gallery to the ante-chamber of King's Chamber. Mr. Smyth thus proceeds :—

" That floor-line, so far from ceasing at the south wall of the Gallery, passes onward from thence through a narrow opening, but on the very same level, to further spaces and further times, entering first of all a very low passage-way leading directly south. Only 53 inches long is this passage, while it is at the same time lower in height than any pyramid passage yet passed through from the very beginning. Wherefore, if the oppressions of idolatry, and the primitive force of war, in the early history of man were symbolised by the cramped-up attitude of any human being in passing through the very first, or pre-Abrahamic passage, which is only 47 inches in transverse, and 53 in vertical height, what shall be represented by the 44 inches only of this small, and last, or post-grand gallery passage? Can it be anything else than the unexampled days of future trouble which the Saviour Himself announced should immediately precede this second, but which must as certainly succeed the dispensation of His first, coming?"

That is, though 1881-2 will be the date of the millennium, 1934-5 will be the year of the absolute descent of Christ upon earth again; but the last fifty-three years will be of great sorrow.

The saints are, however, to be saved these fifty-three years of dire calamity. A way for their escape is made. They are to be caught up to heaven first. And where is this to be symbolised in the pyramid? The key, as usual, fits the lock precisely. The reader has learned before that over the King's Chamber is the rude Construction Chamber, known as Davison's. To this Caviglia found an approach from a curious hole in the Gallery, accessible only by a ladder. It is to this the professor alludes below:—

"Where the Grand Gallery terminates at the 1881-2 southern end, and a distressingly low passage begins, testifying, probably, to times of difficulty and oppression to follow, there is a very peculiar mode of escape or exit from the upper (or near the ceiling) corner of that southern or 1881-2 end of the Grand Gallery. No less than a small concealed passage-way, far over the heads of all travellers below, and leading to a sort of sanctuary over the ceiling of the King's Chamber, the final end of all the historical series of chambers and passages in the building.

" It (the sanctuary above the King's Chamber) is not a place for living human beings, or any walking bodies, the floor being all up and down in huge knobs of granite, and the height too small; but the ceiling of it is exquisitely smooth and true, in polished red granite, and of the same length and breadth as the ceiling of the King's Chamber below.

" There is nothing known in theories of the Great Pyramid that can pretend to explain that strange exit from the upper corner of the Grand Gallery, 28 feet above its floor, and that one sort of sanctuary which it leads to *being left thus accessible to winged beings* by the builder; but the sacred theory may point to it as typical of the carrying up to above the clouds of the saints, just before the troubles of Anti-Christ begin."

All this may be a prophecy of Mr. Piazzi Smyth, and not come from the pyramid. It is a remarkable coincidence that the Gallery should be thus 1881-2 pyramid inches long, when some recent calculators of the millennium, dating Daniel's supposed 1260 years from the *Hegira* of Mahomet in 621-2, got that number.

But the date of the millennium is found to vary in each age. During the first century the event was daily and confidently expected, as we learn from the Epistles. The millennium was looked for subsequently whenever there were wars and rumours of wars. The year 1000, the year 1260, passed. People lost the millennial expectation. If Daniel's mystical language, time, time, and half-time, be interpreted to mean 360 years, twice 360, and half of 360, 1260 years are obtained. The question of addition to that amount has long agitated controversialists. As each particular century has fancied its own near the time, the nineteenth century must needs add enough to bring up the 1260 to that epoch. For a time, 600 was the secret number, and many confidently thought 1860 would bring Napoleon as the Anti-Christ. Then, as Mahomet, the supposed false prophet, fled from Mecca in 622, or, as some say, 632, those numbers furnished new data. When, then, Mr. Smyth gets the length of the Gallery, about 1881 inches, he has but to assume the one end for the birth of Christ to gain his required date.

It is true that no interpretation from Daniel had found the said fifty-three years of affliction, though there is a reference to seventy-five. The worthy professor, apparently for the time losing sight of his own fifty-three years, has a happy way of arranging for the seventy-five. He turns thus to Daniel :—

"The difference between the two periods, 1260 and 1335, is sufficient not only to carry the explorer through that passage and into the far larger proportions of the ante-chamber beyond, but into that part of 'it where the construction, in exquisite red granite, begins both in floor, walls, and ceiling."—"In a more precise and particular degree the difference of 1335 and 1260, or 75, will place humanity just so far within the ante-chamber as to come vertically under that chamber's most remarkable "granite leaf" (the *Portcullis*), whose unique position there, lower than the ceiling, and yet far above the floor, would seem to be typical, if of anything known or proclaimed, of the "New Jerusalem descending from on high."

Assuredly, for the builders so to adapt their measurements, as to chronicle the exact time of the "New Jerusalem descending from on high"—always supposing such descent to become literally a fact—would with most persons definitively settle the question of the Divine inspiration of the pyramid.

But the measurements which are so agreeable to the theory of Mr. Smyth are equally favourable to the very dissimilar theories of Messrs. Dufeu, Hekekyan Bey, Agnew, Wild, and Wilson. Each claims the adaptability for himself, ignoring the smiles of the pyramid upon others. That each person should realise especial gratification from the realisation of his "fancies" is no certain argument for their truth.

It is not for us to pronounce any of these well-demonstrated theories doubtful, for it may be an illustration of the doctrine that there is "not one infallibility, but several infallibilities." After all, too, this may be only an instance of what is recorded about truth being many-sided.

The millennial teaching of the pyramid is dwelt upon by Mr. Harrison Oxley, who sees that "the fashion and the measurement were sacred and heavenly, and, therefore, Divine." The prophetical character of the building is thus described :—

"It is the altar and the pillar foretold by the prophet (Isa. xix. 19, 20), but also 'the temple of God' to be measured as given to the beloved disciple in Revelation (Rev. xi. 1, 2). Moreover, it must be a temple that should be in existence long after several of the great events in the Christian dispensation had transpired. Where are we to look for this temple? It must not be an idolatrous or heathen temple ; such temples belong to Satan, and not to God. They have no measure, according to the rule of God's Word. ' The temple of God' to be measured was not at Jerusalem, because it was doomed to fall." The temple must be that set in the border of Egypt.

He proceeds :—" The Great Pyramid has been measured, and it comes forth as a witness and a sign. It is a witness to Moses and the prophets, to Christ and the apostles, therefore to the truth of Divine revelation, therefore to the Lord of Hosts."—"It is found not to be a profane, but a sacred building; not of human origin, but Divine. By its locality it answers to the altar and pillar of the Lord of Hosts, spoken of by the prophet Isaiah, to appear in the latter days. By its measurement it corresponds to the temple of God and the altar recorded by the beloved disciple in Revelation."

The pyramid is said to be a sacred edifice, because it was built by Divine inspiration, and it bears the record of piety in being, unlike temples, without idolatrous emblems.

That this may be an error of judgment is apparent from the fact that the Great Pyramid, like all other pyramids, is situated in the midst of a Necropolis, abounding with idolatrous emblems, containing tombs of officers belonging to the Court of Cheops, the very builder himself, and all such tombs having addresses to heathen deities. In the pyramid itself the quarry marks of the king's name are distinctly idolatrous emblems. The same persons whose names are therein inscribed are elsewhere spoken of in tablets as being worshippers of false gods, and the constructors of idols of gold, &c., for the adornment of a temple. It is simply a delusion, therefore, to speak of the pyramid being a witness of religious truth, although coincidences favour a theory.

Mr. James Simpson still further extends the millennial idea, dwelling upon the Jewish parallelism. "Counting in natural years," he says, "Israel will hold her seventieth jubilee in A.D. 2000; but, counting in prophetic years, 1950. Or, according to the former, her great jubilee will extend from A.D. 1931 to 2000 inclusive; but, according to the latter, from 1882 to 1950 inclusive. Thus the Great Pyramid date, 1881-2, turns up again, and with a more distinctly defined meaning, by using the undoubtedly Scriptural number 360." He adds, "And although the forty-nine years from 1881 to 1930 may thus partake of the character of a Great Sabbath to Israel, the period following, or from 1931 to 2000, will be the true jubilee."

This will fit in with the Zoroastrian doctrine laid down in Persia hundreds of years before Daniel. According to the ancient Persians, the regeneration of the world would take place in 2000, when the serpent Azis-Dahaka is to be chained a thousand years. The same was believed by the ancient Chaldeans, Egyptians, Odin-worshippers, and Druids. The chained serpent is found in the four divisions of the world. One may see it on the sarcophagus of the Soane Museum in Lincoln's Inn Fields. But it may be assumed by some that these millennial myths, so widely found, originated from the Inspired Pyramid. Is it not strange that while the heathen nations cherished the hope of this millennium, the Jews were left in so much darkness about it by Moses, David, and the prophets?

A singular pyramid controversy has sprung up about the Millennial date of 1881-2. Those who had received the conjectured Divine indication of the Grand Gallery, and had been quietly looking forward to some four years of peace before the stirring catastrophe, have been somewhat disturbed by an announcement that chronology is at fault, and that this year is absolutely 1881, and not 1877.

But this is no novel discovery. Every book of chronology is seen, in a most curious way, to show that our Saviour was born in the *year* 4, though we reckon our year of the Lord four years before. Mystics have no difficulty about the matter. They can even comprehend how the year may have ten months and yet twelve. But to common-sense eyes there does seem a puzzle.

One Mr. Clark anxiously asks "whether the mistake of four years announced really could have been made in astronomical time and still remain uncorrected?" Prof. Piazzi Smyth, appealed to, replies that "they do not, as astronomers, and by dint of accurate astronomical science, pretend to know anything of the date of Christ's birth, they merely take the existing mode of reckoning of years among all the civilised nations. Then, in his letter to the *Life from the Dead*, the Scotch astronomer cautiously writes, "It may be that it is a part of the Divine purposes that this particular point of chronology shall not be fully cleared up until the time of the end itself arises."

The error is supposed to be owing to the monk Dionysius Exequus, to whom we are indebted for the "year of the Lord." In 527, he calculated according to 4713 of the Julian period, supposed to be four years out. It is difficult to correct the monk after 1350 years, especially when mysticism manufactured dates, without reference to real events. But Mr. Cockburn-

Muir is positive the monk was correct, and he can prove it *by the pyramid.*

A Mr. Chapman writes :—" Dr. Hales (the *chronologist*) says the difference of opinion respecting the precise period of the birth of Christ arises from the fact that this era was not used until so many centuries had elapsed that it was *almost impossible* with any accuracy to fix the date." Canon Farrar, in his *Life of Christ,* considers this year 1881, and not 1877. If he and the pyramid are to be believed, the millennium may be expected within a few months.

Having discussed both the astronomical and religious teaching of the pyramid, other scientific and mystical instruction may now be indicated.

36. THE RISE AND FALL OF LAND IN EGYPT.

So dependent were the people upon the inundation of the Nile that everything connected therewith was invested with supreme importance. The heliacal rising of Sirius, the Dog-star, indicating the approaching elevation of the river, occasioned that star, or the deity it represented, to become an object of worship.

As may readily be imagined, the elevation or depression of the soil of the country, in relation to the surface of the Nile itself, or the level of the Mediterranean and Red Seas, would be most carefully and constantly observed. Upon that depended the spread of the water annually over the fields, filling canals and reservoirs. The excess of overflow may be as unwelcome as the diminution of supply. All parts of the world, as geologists now inform us, are in a more or less disturbed state, rising or falling. The learned priests of Egypt were aware of this fact seven thousand or more years ago, when they constructed the first canals and reservoirs, and rescued the valley of the Nile from alternate drought and marshy desolation.

M. Hekekyan Bey, C. E., of Constantinople and Cairo, has paid much attention to this subject in his remarkable work of 1863 on *The Chronology of the Siriadic Monuments.* The chief of these monuments are pyramids and obelisks. Only a glance at the question can be spared, but intelligent readers are directed to the volume for complete information.

He considers that the constructors of all pyramids, obelisks, sphinxes, and temples regulated their elevation, at the epoch of erection, to the level of the adjoining seas. At any subsequent period the wise priests could, by means of instruments long lost to view, ascertain from the relation borne by the Red Sea, at a fixed spot, or by the Mediterranean, to the platform or ideal apex of the Great Pyramid, whether the country were in an ascendant or descendant condition. Upon the settlement of this question, adequate measures would be taken with canals and embankments to prevent any evil consequences from a change, or provide for any prospective difference of level. There is reason to believe that in the valley of the Indus and the valley of the Ganges, if not even that of the Oxus, similar measures were adopted by the professing priests, but real scientific professors, of the past.

"The hypogeum of the First Pyramid," writes Hekekyan Bey, "was fixed 5' to the west, and about 2' to the south, of the Niloscope station (lat 30° 1' 7"). It was situated on the right bank of the river, and had the limestone rock of the Mokattam for its solid foundation. The reason why that spot was chosen is most important. While the van of the annual torrents of the Nile habitually reached the Memphis and Heliopolis parallels in the period of the summer solstice, the secular amplitude of the torrents in the maximum state of development, or the difference between the lowest ebb and the highest flood-levels of the river, measured exactly fifteen standard Nile cubits in the parallel of the observatory, and the Osirtasic ordinate of the river in the same parallel, or the vertical supposed to connect the lowest secular ebb of the Erythræan Sea (the Red Sea) during the autumnal equinoxes at Clysma (port near Suez) and the secular maximum flood-level of the Nile in the Niloscopic parallel, measured forty-two cubits and a half of the Sothis scale."

In another place he points out changes which have occurred.

" The summit of the First Pyramid was (*in the design*) elevated 118·140 noctas above the high Nile level, in B.C. 4863, the date of its hidrymatisation; it is now 111·588 noctas above the same hydraulic level, and will be submerged, with the subsidence of the crust of the earth on which it is solidly founded, in 111·41 noctas ·of time, or Nile years, before any of its geometrical records can have time to be destroyed by the action of the elements, and, remaining preserved in the bowels of the earth, will again emerge to light in a state as perfect as that of the diminutive sea-shell now found embedded in the summits of high mountain ranges, and will in proper time reveal to the human race the science of their constructors, and teach them useful lessons for their guidance, and, should they have forgotten it, teach them the existence of a Great Maker of the makers of these curious monuments."

M. Dufeu, the author of that exhaustive book of learning the *Quatre Pyramides de Gizeh*, declares that "the most important among the principal and numerous distinctions of the Great Pyramid " is " *to establish and preserve eternally the perfect knowledge of the hydraulic level of the Nile and the valley, in relation to the lowest level of the Red Sea.*"

He divides the results obtained by "this precious monument" into two categories :—" 1. *Chronologiques, chronologico-astronomiques et historiques.* 2. *Hydraulico-geologiques, géodésiques et geographiques.*" The present subject, affecting hydraulics, would come under the last head. He admits the suppositious enquiry, but wisely remarks, " It is often by hypothesis that we arrive at certainty."

After referring to the very interesting and suggestive subject of Manetho's *anonymous* dynasties, as contrasted with those in which the names of kings were given, he writes as follows :—

"The coincidence of these anonymous dynasties with the epochs of two movements of elevation, the most approved of which Egypt has been the theatre, had struck us, and made us think that perhaps they signified the epochs of geological rising, which in that case would authorise the non-anonymous dynasties as indicating the periods of depression, may be, of sinking of the soil; now, having applied this system to the movement, which appears simultaneous to us, the elevation which has raised at first the level of the Nile, at the second cataract, to seven metres above the highest actual waters, under the twelfth and thirteenth dynasties, and at the epoch of the

Exodus divided the Red Sea from the Bitter Lakes, and taking
for the base of our calculations the normal measure of sinking
as of elevation of the soil of the Nile valley, represented by the
length of the *Nilometric cubit* divided in 360 parts, or metric
noctas, equivalent to those crises in 360 years, we have almost
acquired the certainty that our idea was just and our opinion
well founded. But this certainty becomes complete when, applying the same system in an inverse sense, that is to say, the
measures of the depression of the soil indicated by the non-
anonymous dynasties to the result of the survey made in 1837
by Perring, we have found the same measure as he between the
base of the Great Pyramid and the Nile at its level."

It should be understood that in geodesic formula the Nilometric cubit has the value of a degree; but, employed numeric-
ally, the value of a nocta.

In this he finds a confirmation of "the sinking of the soil,
at least in the locality of the pyramids, and an approach between
the base of the monument and the lowest level of the Red Sea,
since the time of the construction of the Great Pyramid down
to our own day." And thus does he put the matter simply :—

" The Egyptian wise men, to whom were confided the destinies
of the country, had connected the hydraulic levels of the river
with different plans or sections of the vertical height of the
pyramid, giving to it, from the base to the summit, an elevation
which, added to that of the ordinary level and the maximum of
the increase of the current, above the level of the sea, might determine the constant height of these two hydraulic levels, by a
connection with that of the maritime level taken as place of
comparison, and made them serve thus as an eternal hydraulic

and geological sign for the operations of surveying—operations indispensable for the regulation of the annual alluviums of the Nile in its bed and in its valley."

37. TO ILLUSTRATE GEOMETRIC TRUTH.

The square and the triangle, with their several properties, together with the relation of diameter and circumference, as well as the correspondence of the radius of a circle and the side of a square, are all well brought before the intelligent eye in the pyramid.

Mr. H. C. Agnew, in a work published 1838, says, "The pyramids of Egypt appear in general to have been emblems of the sacred sphere and its great circle exhibited in the most convenient architectural form. The chief objects of these buildings being to serve for sepulchral monuments, the Egyptians sought in the appropriate figure of the pyramid to perpetuate at the same time a portion of their geometrical science."

This gentleman was, perhaps, the first to point out an interesting mathematical discovery. "The Third Pyramid," said he, "was the spirit of this holy *circle*, since it defined the *square equal to it in perimeter* and in area by showing the *difference between their sides and the diameter of the circle.*"

38. TO SHOW THE PROPORTION OF DIAMETER AND CIRCUMFERENCE.

Mr. John Taylor, in *The Great Pyramid: why was it built?* lays down the proposition that the vertical height is to the double of its base as the diameter is to the circumference of a circle. This question is dependent on the angle made by the face of the pyramid with its base.

The slope angle has been more accurately determined since the discovery of the casing-stones by Col. Vyse in 1837. Mr. Taylor speaks of 51° 49′ 46″, and Mr. Smyth of 51° 51′ 14″. That slope with a certain base establishes the so-called *Rho* theory (π), the proportion of diameter to circumference, 3·14159. Archimedes made it 3·14286. The Hindoos' *Vija Ganita*, of 3927 to 1250, brings out 3·1416. On this Mr. Taylor remarks, "The Hindoo proportion is identical with that, so far as its numbers go, which was expressed in English inches when the pyramids were founded." While the real amount is 3·1415927, he obtains 3·141792 from the pyramid. He thinks no other pyramid has so true a relation.

The Queen's Chamber has a niche. This, 185 inches, multiplied by 10 and then by 3·14159, yields 5812, the vertical height of the pyramid. The wall of the chamber, 182·62 pyramid inches, multiplied by 100 and divided by 2, will show 9131 for the side of the pyramid in pyramid inches.

Prof. Piazzi Smyth utilises the *Rho* theory in connection with the King's Chamber, to get the length of a cubit, saying, "On being simply computed according to the modern determination of the value of π, and length of the year, and comes out from the local measure of 412·545 British inches to be 25·0250 + British inches."

Although an ingenious discovery, and admitted by Sir John Herschel, this latter distinguished man adds, "We are not entitled to conclude that they (the Egyptians) were aware of this coincidence (3·14159), and intended to embody both results in their building."

Sir Edmund Beckett calls attention to the assumed 11 to 7

theory; that, with the slope of 51° 51′ 14″, the width is to the height as the length of a quadrant is to its radius. He does not think with Mr. Smyth and others that this was a primary motive of construction, " though," says he, "they did use it for fixing the size, probably taking it approximately from the slopes."

He shows that with the angle at 51° 50′ the height is a mean proportional between the length down the middle of each slope and half the width of the base. The 51° he esteems "about the slope at which mounds of earth will stand naturally." He points out another singular coincidence. The diagonal angle at the top, 96°, or four times 24°, would equal that of the four sectors of a quindecagon. (Euclid, iv. 10, 11, 16.)

The parallelism is exhibited in the coffer, whose height is to the two adjacent sides as the diameter is to the circumference.

Captain Tracey, taking for the radius of a circle the height of the pyramid, 232·52 cubits, pyramid measure, finds the diameter bear the same proportion to the periphery of a square whose side is 365·243, the length of the base in cubits, or days in a year, as 1 is to 3·1416. With 412·132, the length of the King's Chamber in inches, as the diameter, the circle would equal a square whose side, 365·242, in cubits, measures the base of the pyramid.

"Never have any monuments," says M. Dufeu, "exercised the sagacity of the learned as the pyramids of Gizeh."

39. TO MASONIFY THE QUADRATURE OF THE CIRCLE.

Mr. H. C. Agnew conceives that one purpose of the erection was to masonify approximately the relation of square and circle.

" Here we find," writes he, " the *quadrature of the circle* exemplified in a curious manner, with all practicable approach and correctness, by the Egyptians." He, however, admits that " its arithmetical solution is known now to be impossible; the geometrical solution, in all probability, is so likewise; but whether the Egyptian priests were of this opinion I cannot venture to say."

Only a few quotations can be given from his publication, just sufficient to indicate his object :—

" If a square described about a circle be conceived to be drawn up from the centre in the form of a pyramid, having the perpendicular equal to the radius of a circle, and the superficies of the square be supposed to adjust itself equally among the planes of the four isosceles triangles of the faces of the pyramid, each face of such pyramid will, of course, be equal in area to one quarter of the square, or equal to the square of the radius; and the new square formed by the four lines of the bases of the triangles of the faces of the pyramid will be equal in perimeter to the circumference of the circle, with an error in excess of about one part in fourteen hundred."

" In the original diagram we find the proportion of five to four very dominant; the diameter of the circle is five, and that of the great square four, and thence, of course, the perpendicular of the pyramid is to half its base as five to four."

" If the tangent be to the radius as five to four the angle is 51° 20' 25", and this being so very near the result of my observations, I am justified in concluding that the perpendicular of the Great Pyramid was to half its base as five to four, or to its base as five to eight."

" Two perpendiculars, being radii of circles, are together equal to the sum of the perimeters of the bases."

He was particularly emphatic in his observations forty years ago upon the superiority of the *Third* Pyramid. Its true angle is affirmed to be 51° 51' 14", and this, adds he, would be "a perfection which neither of the two great pyramids separately possessed; namely, that *its perpendicular was the radius of a circle, the circumference of which was equal to the square of its base.*"

He concludes with this statement :—" The Third Pyramid appears to be an emanation (if I may so say) from the first great principle of the system, the circle of origin, of which it is the spirit or essence."

Hekekyan Bey of Constantinople holds a similar high conception of the Third Pyramid, saying, " Of the Siriadic monuments erected in the land of Egypt, hers was considered to be the richest in scientific records, and the most perfect; it was, also, the most beautiful from its high ornamentation, being of a ruddy complexion, from its exterior casing of polished granite."

Sir Henry James brings out a similar result to that shown by Mr. Taylor first. He speaks of a pyramid rising at the corners nine to ten as a π pyramid, and its height being equal to the radius of a circle whose circumference is very approximately equal to the length of the four sides of the base." The height $486 \times 2 \times 3.1416 = 3053.6$. But four times the length, 764, $= 3056$.

A curious thing is noted respecting the floor of the Antechamber. The granite part is, according to Mr. Casey, 103.03 pyramid inches, and the limestone 116.26 inches. Taking the first as the side of a square, and the last as the diameter of a circle, the areas of the two figures will be about equal. The side of the base, 9131 inches, is obtained by $116 \cdot 26 \times 3 \cdot 1416 \times 5 \times 5$. Also, $116 \cdot 26 \times 50$ courses from the base to the Ante-chamber $= 5813$, the apex height of the pyramid; but, $103 \cdot 03 \times 50 = 5151 \cdot 65$. Taking this as the side of the square, the area will equal that of a triangle of the shape and size of the pyramid's vertical meridian section, and to a circle having the height of the pyramid for its diameter.

Captain Tracey, taking the length of the coffer in pyramid inches, $412 \cdot 132$, as the diameter, finds the circle to equal a square whose side is the base of the pyramid in cubits; but $412 \cdot 132$ as the square side will bring an equal circle area with the radius of the height of the pyramid, $232 \cdot 52$ cubits. The pyramid inches inside the King's Chamber equal, to the thousandth part, the sacred cubits outside. The diameter of a circle with $232 \cdot 52$ for a radius is to the periphery of a square whose side is $365 \cdot 242$ as 1 is to $3 \cdot 1416$.

40. A PART OF A GREAT PYRAMIDAL SYSTEM.

Instead of being isolated in its grandeur and peculiarities, Mr. Agnew believes the three larger pyramids were associated by construction in one geometrical plan. Prof. Smyth and others have remarked upon the difference of angle made by the face with the plane of the base; and, noting certain mathematical data along with the angle of the Great Pyramid, have concluded that edifice to have a special distinction. But Mr. H. C. Agnew, after giving the angle of the first, 51° 20′ 1″, of the second 52° 25′ 51″, and of the third, 51° 51′, calls the last "the most perfect geometrical figure."

"If," says he, "the deductions of the following pages be

admitted, we must arrive at the remarkable conclusion that the *three great pyramids of Gizeh were component parts of one immense system.*"

He proceeds, " How must our wonder be increased when we find that all were planned at once ! that before a stone of the great causeway was laid the precise proportions of the Second and Third Pyramids, as well as of the First, were unalterably determined by the necessary effect of the rule which fixed the length and breadth of the causeway itself ! " He adds, " I believe the works of the Second Pyramid were begun long before the First Pyramid was completed, and the Third had probably risen high above the ground before the summit of the second was carried to a point."

This is not the place to elaborate his principle, but there is much to draw us toward it. The Egyptians were a supremely geometrical people. In their national edifices the learned rulers were not governed by a simple idea of beauty, nor of ordinary practical utility with beauty. We, in our day, would raise a museum, a gallery of arts, a House of Parliament, or a cathedral, adapted for the specific object intended to be carried out, combining with that as much architectural elegance as particular tastes suggest, though mainly derived from the adoption of the style of some older building. We should contemplate nothing further. There would be no design of incorporating any symbolism, leave alone the introduction of mathematical and scientific truths.

But we are well assured, on the contrary, that philosophical minds presided at national constructions beside the Nile some five or six thousand years ago. These were not raised merely to excite the wonder of the ignorant, or please the imagination of the refined. They were not for the petty gratification of the builder, or the adornment of his own age. A purpose, distinct and important, was before the mind. There was something to be remembered, something to be taught. A truism was to be perpetuated in a form more enduring than letters, more faithful in its teaching than words. We are gradually arriving at the conviction that these wise master-masons worked upon a plan, philosophical and true, and in a way that emulated the eternity of the truth itself.

Apart from being an illustration of the learning of the Egyptians, there are reasons which make Mr. Agnew's theory at least feasible.

It is in harmony with the building mind of the Egyptians, who had a system of thought, and were working toward it. The identity of construction seems apparent in the family likeness of the Gizeh group, not noticed elsewhere, in their relative positions, and in the formation of the *one* causeway described by Herodotus, the remains of which we behold. Though this theory injures the overruling supremacy of the Great Pyramid believed in by some others, it is a pleasing recognition of the far-seeing, truth-telling, science-following qualities of the ancient Egyptians.

But Mr. John James Wild, in his celebrated letter to Lord Brougham in 1850, was perhaps the first to recognise the scientific relation of one pyramid to the other, in the group at Gizeh. Whatever priority there be in the First Pyramid, he is of opinion that all are related in one harmonious whole. His conclusion is thus stated : "There exists a certain proportion between the elevations of the bases of the three great pyramids of Gizeh which proves anew that science has presided at the erection of these monuments."

His calculations are based upon the cubit of Sir Isaac Newton and Mr. Greaves, or cubit of Memphis, and not that of Messrs. Taylor and Smyth.

He contends that the Second and the Third Pyramids exhibit the *law of the retrogradation of the ascendant node of the equator in the ecliptic.*

The entrance of the Second Pyramid is $25\frac{1}{2}$ cubits to the east of the centre. Taking the Memphis cubit, now in Paris,—found by Vyse and Perring to be, according to the French measurement, 522 millemètres, and divided in twenty-eight equal parts, —Mr. Wild ascertains that in twenty-five and a half days the ascendant node retrogrades 206 cubits on the equator; this 206 is exactly the length of the *Third* Pyramid. Dividing 206 by 28, and then multiplying by the annual diminution, as given by Maëdler, 0·4758, the result is 3·5″ for the equator indication But 3·5″, or 206 cubits, would be the base of the *Third* Pyramid.

Now the base of the second is double that of the third. This, as is seen, was designed by the builders at one period. If the one is 206, the other is 412 cubits base. But the centre is $25\frac{1}{2}$ from the entrance, therefore one side would be $180\frac{1}{2}$ and the other $231\frac{1}{2}$. The difference is 51. Mr. Wild then says, " In fifty-one days the ascendant node retrogrades 412 cubits." But this will be twice 3·5″, the length of the *Third* Pyramid, or 7″, which is the exact base of the Second.

The yearly retrogradation will be $365\frac{1}{4}$ divided by 51, and that amount multiplied by 7″. The product is 50·13″. The ascendant node, therefore, completes its course of retrogression in 25,852 years, or 360° divided by 50·13″. Astronomers, who are not agreed as to the precession of the equinoxes, rate it between 50·1″ and 50·2″, or from 25,817 to 25,888 years. The Egyptians, in the pyramids of Gizeh, struck between those dates, or not far from the Hindoo year of the gods, 25,920 years.

Again, the Second and Third Pyramids conjointly perpetuate the duration of the tropical year. The base of the Third Pyramid is 41′ 7″ above the base of the Great Pyramid, while that of the second is 33′ 2″ above it. The difference is 8′ 5″, equal to 4·9 cubits. This added to the elevation of the second above the Nile, 100, equals 104·9. Add this result to the elevation of the Third, 128 cubits, and we have 232·9. The maximum of the tropical year is $365\frac{232.9}{24 \times 40}$. In forty years there are $14600\frac{232.9}{24}$ days. Upon this he writes, "In forty years there remain a number of intercalary days which is equal to the number of cubits contained in the elevation of the summit of the Third Pyramid above the level of the Nile (232·9), divided by the number of cubits contained in the elevation of the Second Pyramid above the level of the same (24), namely, $\frac{232.9}{24} = 9\frac{16.9}{24}$, or $9\frac{169}{240}$ intercalary days."

Suppose the civil year equal to 365 days, twenty-four years present 8760 days. The same number (8760) in seconds is equal to 146′ or 2° 26′; and if this be taken from the latitude 30° we obtain 27° 24′. This, according to Perring, is the inclination of the interior passage of the Third Pyramid. It had previously been shown that in 500 years the tropics retrograded 238 seconds. But this is the number of cubits on the western side of the entrance of the Great Pyramid. If 238′, or 3° 58′, be taken from 30° the result is 26° 2′, the angle of inclination of the entrance passage of the Third Pyramid.

Mr. Wild has another remarkable parallel, or *coincidence*, as some may prefer to call it.

As before mentioned, the base of the Second Pyramid is 7″, and of the third 3·5″. The square of the Second Pyramid's base is 49″. If the centre of the base of this pyramid be taken for the centre of a circle, and a regular polygon of forty-nine sides be inscribed therein, the central angle of the polygon will be 7° 20′ 48$\frac{4}{4}\frac{8}{9}$″. This doubled is 14° 41′ 37$\frac{4}{4}\frac{7}{9}$″, which equals $\frac{360°}{3·5 \times 7}$; this is, says he, " equal to the number of degrees of the circumference of a circle, divided by the product of the numbers of meridian seconds contained in the bases of the Second and Third Pyramids."

Again, he goes on to say, " According to Colonel Howard Vyse, the base of the Third Pyramid is 8′ 5″ above the base of the Second, and that of the Second is 33′ 2″ above the base of the Great Pyramid. Now the proportion between the elevation of the base of the Second Pyramid above the base of the Great, and the elevation of the base of the Third Pyramid above the base of the Second, is equal to the proportion between the radius and the sinus of 14° 41′ 37$\frac{4}{4}\frac{7}{9}$ = 33′ 2″ to 8′ 5″; that is, equal to the proportion between the radius and sinus of the double of the central angle of a polygon which has as many sides as the square of the base of the Second Pyramid contains square seconds, namely 49."

The eighteen years' lunar period is also obtained by relation of Gizeh pyramids.

The base of the Second is 7″, which squared and multiplied by

5, the pyramid number, yields 245″. Subtracting this from the latitude 30° we have 25° 55′—the inclination of the interior passage of the Second Pyramid. The inclination of the lower entrance of the Second is 22° 15′, which taken from 30°, leaves 7° 45′, or 465′. But 465 years will be 25 lunar cycles, of $18\frac{3}{5}$ each. Again, the base of the most southern of the three pyramids to the east of the great one is 93 cubits; making, in years, 5 lunar cycles.

Once more. He says that "the base of the three pyramids south of the Third are lower than the base of the Third, 16′ 18″. Consequently, the bases of the three pyramids are lower than the base of the Second Pyramid as many feet as the base of the Third is above the base of the Second. The levels of the bases of the Third and the three pyramids, therefore, form two tangents of a circle of which the radius is equal to the sinus of the double central angle of the above-mentioned polygon. When each side of the heptagon contains twice 28 cubits, namely, twice the amount of cubits of the retrogradation of the tropic during one year, the circumference of the circle inscribed in the heptagon measures $365\frac{28}{99}$ cubits, or as many cubits as one year contains days."

Lastly :—The entrance of the Second Pyramid is 24 cubits above the base, and the top is 267. The entrance above the Nile is 100 + 24. "If we add," says Mr. Wild, "the 100 cubits of elevation of the base of the Second Pyramid above the level of the Nile to the 412 cubits contained in this base, we obtain $100 + 412 = 512 = 2^9$ cubits. Now 512 years contain as many intercalary days as there are cubits in the elevation of the entrance of the Second Pyramid above the level of the Nile, namely 124. Consequently, 512 years contain $(512 \times 365) + 124$ $= 187,004$ days. As before mentioned, the summit of the Second Pyramid is 367, which equals $365 + 2$, cubits above the level of the Nile. The civil year, taken at 365 days, leaves a surplus of two intercalary days after a lapse of $\frac{1024}{124} = \frac{1000}{100} + \frac{24}{24}$ $= 8\frac{8}{31}$ years. But in 2^7, 128, years, or in as many years as the vertical height of the Third Pyramid contains cubits, there remains as many intercalary days as the fourth part of the elevation of the entrance of the Second Pyramid above the level of the Nile contains cubits, namely, $\frac{124}{4}$ or 31 intercalary days." He thus obtains, in 128 years, $(128 \times 365) + 31 = 46,751$ days. The average length of a tropical year is ascertained by these two pyramids, and by the Memphis cubit, to be $365\frac{31}{128}$ days.

By another calculation, founded upon the three pyramids south of the Third Pyramid, he obtains the result of $365\frac{88}{99}$.

The author of the *Solar System of the Ancients*, as well as M. Dufeu, and other writers, confirm the opinion of Mr. Wild, that the pyramids of Gizeh were constructed upon one plan, and that they form a truly family group.

41. AGREEMENT WITH THE CAUSEWAY.

According to Mr. Agnew's mathematical plan, "the Great Causeway was in length equal to the circumference of the chief circle, or parent of the whole scheme, that of which the First Pyramid was radius, and of which the square of the base of the Second Pyramid was the inscriptible square. The Causeway was the circumference rolled out, as it were."

If the perpendicular of the pyramid be 480 feet, the circumference of the circle would be 3016. Estimating a stadium at

603 feet, he obtains 3015 for the length of the five stadia of Herodotus, given as the extent of the Causeway.

"I believe," says Mr. Agnew, "this Great Causeway led up to the eastern side of the Great Pyramid, and terminated in front at 159 feet from the base, or at the eastern verge of the circle descriptible about the base."

The width of the Causeway was 62 Greek feet. Upon this he remarks that if the radius of the inner circle, 1000, be subtracted from that of the outer, 1131·3698, half the difference between the two rings would be about 62½ ; this nearly corresponds with the width of the Causeway.

42. TO TYPIFY THE GENERATIVE PRINCIPLE.

There has been a time in the history of the world when a Babel confusion existed through the contention of two parties : one holding the masculine origin of being, and the other the feminine. Certain nations, as the Phœnicians, Greeks, &c., favoured the latter in their forms of worship ; in Peru, Britain, &c., it was the former. India has for ages been the scene of this religious strife. The enormous popularity of Siva proclaims the triumph at last of the masculine principle there.

The pyramid is said to typify the same thing as the conical stone worshipped in so many lands, and from the remotest period. The revolution of a pyramid describes a cone. The cone represents the Phallic theory of creation.

A mystic, the Chevalier de B——, thus connects the astronomical and Phallic ideas :—"Its apex represents the Phallus, the sign ever deemed throughout the East the symbol of Deity, or the *creative principle*. The descent of the sun upon its apex at the two solemn epochs of the year (equinoxes), which signify life eternal, and death through the ever-constant adverse principle of evil, completes the series of allegorical ideas which this building was designed to celebrate."

But he suggestively reminds us that while the number *one* shows the masculine principle, and *three* the feminine, *four* illustrates the harmony of both. " Its base," says he, " is the perfect square, which symbolises in its four corners the sacred number *four*, the union of the masculine and feminine principles." The scholar is reminded of the *speaking* numbers of Pythagoras and of the Cabbala.

In the above sense it is held that the pyramid is the most simple and suggestive type of creative force, and the conjunction of both active and passive agencies in the operations of Divine mind on matter. This is a large question, but must be abruptly closed.

43. EMBLEM OF THE SUN OR SACRED FIRE.

The shape of the pyramids has suggested that of *tongues of fire*. To Jablonski it appeared as sunbeams streaming down from a point. Mr. Wild, of Zurich, calls attention to the tradition that they were erected to the sun. Mr. Yeates truly remarks that they are a just imitation of fire. Syncellus informs us that Venephres built the pyramids of Co-chone. Bryant finds *Co-chone* to mean the house of Chon, the sun; " which," says he, " seems to betray the purpose for which the chief pyramid was erected ; for it was undoubtedly nothing else but a monument to the deity whose name it bore." As it had been called *Domus Opis Serpentis,* the learned man remarks,

"It was the name of the pyramid erected to the sun, the Ophite deity of Egypt, worshipped under the symbol of a serpent."

Arab writers are of this opinion. Soyuti, who died 911 A.H., says that the Sabæans, or fire-worshippers, "in performing pilgrimages to the pyramids sacrificed hens and black calves." He quotes Menardi to prove that Hermes, the son of Seth, introduced Sabæanism, inculcating the necessity of such pilgrimages. Makrizi, 845 A.H., quotes Ibrahim Alwatwati and others upon the sun subject. Al Akbari confirms the tradition. Col. Chesney declares that there are pyramids in Syria to which pilgrimages are still made. Sprenger quotes the story of the model of a pyramid being the object of adoration among the Calmuks.

The religious significance of the pyramid is alluded to by the old English astronomer, Greaves. He thinks the Egyptians may have "intended to represent some of their gods." "For," he adds, "anciently both theye and some others of the Gentiles by columnes and obeliskes did so. Whereas a pyramid is but a greater kinde of obeliske."

An extract from Pierius is given by Mr. Greaves :—

"By a pyramid the ancient Egyptians expressed the nature of things, and that informed substance receiving all forms. Because, as a pyramid, having its beginning from a point on the top, is by degrees dilated on all parts, so the nature of all things proceeding from one fountain and beginning, which is indivisible, namely, from God, the chief workmaster, afterwards receives several forms, and is diffused into various kinds and species, all which it conjoins to that beginning and point, from whence everything issues and flows. There may be also given another reason for this, taken from astronomy, for the Egyptians were excellent astronomers, even the inventors of it. These will have each sign of the zodiac to be a kind of pyramid, the base of which shall be in the heaven, and the point of it shall be in the centre of the earth. Seeing, therefore, in these pyramids all things were made, and that the coming of the sun, which is, as it were, a point in respect of these signs, is the cause of the production of natural things, and its departure the cause of their corruption, it seems very fitly that by a pyramid, Nature, the parent of all things, may be expressed. Also, the same Egyptians, under the form of a pyramid, shadowed forth the soul of man, making huge pyramids the magnificent sepulchres of their kings and heroes, to testify that the soul was still existent, notwithstanding the body was dissolved and corrupted, the which shall generate and produce another body for itself, when it should seem good to the First Agent (that is, the circle of 36,000 years being transacted). Like as a pyramid, as is well known to geometricians, the top of it standing fixed, and the base being moved about, describes a circle, and the whole body of it a cone, so that the circle expresses that space of years, and the cone that body which in that space is produced. For it was the opinion of the Egyptians that in the revolution of 36,000 years all things should be restored to their former estate. Plato witnesses that he received it from them; who seems, also, in his *Timæus* to attest this thing, that is, that our soul has the form of a pyramid, which (soul), according to the same Plato, is of a fiery nature, and adheres to the body as a pyramid does to its base, as a fire does to the fuel."

M. Rougé, last year, said, "The Great Pyramids were the

tombs of kings, but their exact orientation leads us to suppose that they were put in relation with the worship of the sun. Our Votive Pyramids confirm these characters. The principal personage is usually figured in adoration, the face turned toward the south; at his left were the formulas of invocation to the rising sun, and at the right were analogous formulas of invocation to the setting sun."

From Mr. Stewart, of America, we have further remarks. He notes the appearance of the sun about the time of the equinoxes. Twice a year the pyramid would have no shadow. "The sun," says he, "would then appear exactly at midday upon the summit of this pyramid; there his majestic disk would appear, *for some moments*, placed upon this immense pedestal, and seem to *rest* upon it, while his worshippers, on their knees at its base, extending their view along the inclined plane of the northern front, would contemplate the great Osiris, as well when he descended into the darkness of the tomb as when he arose triumphant. The same might be said of the full moon of the equinoxes, when it takes place in this parallel. It would seem that the Egyptians, always grand in their conceptions, had executed a project (the boldest that was ever imagined) of giving a pedestal to the sun and moon, or to Osiris and Isis. The tomb of Osiris was covered with shade nearly six months, after which light surrounded it entirely at midday, as soon as he, returning from *hell*, regained his empire in passing into the luminous atmosphere. Then he had returned to Isis, and to the god of spring, Orus, who had at length conquered the genius of darkness and of winter. What a sublime idea!"

Mr. Fellows, author of *Mysteries of Freemasonry*, takes a

masonic view of the pyramid, giving it a solar worship origin ; or, rather, demonstrating it to have reference to apparent solar movements as well as to solar myths.   He calls the pyramid " a pedestal to the sun and moon, or to Osiris and Isis, at midday for the one, and at midnight for the other, when they arrived at that part of the heavens near to which passes the line which separates the northern from the southern hemisphere, the empire of good from that of evil.   They wished that the shade should disappear from all the fronts of the pyramid at midday, during the whole time that the sun sojourned in the luminous atmosphere, and that the northern front should be again covered with shade when Osiris (the sun) descended into the tomb, or *hell*. The tomb of Osiris was covered with shade nearly six months." As to the fourteen days before one equinox, and after another, Mr. Fellows cites the tradition of masonic Jews, that Hiram's body lay fourteen days in the grave before it was found by Solomon.

The orientation of the pyramid has been held to be a strong confirmation of the solar idea.   Mr. Piazzi Smyth puts it at only 4' 35" of error from true east and west.   Sir Edmund Beckett quotes it 5', or one foot in 761 feet.   But he adds, " It is not quite certain that the ground has not received some slight subsequent twist from below, for the Second Pyramid has exactly the same direction, and, what is more, the whole of the King's Chamber has received a tilt towards one corner, so that the axis of the room is no longer quite vertical."

Even Rollin, in the unenquiring age in which he lived, is so struck with this orientation as to say, " This seems to prove, also, that these immense buildings were never intended exclusively for burial-places, but conjointly for experiment and historical record."

44. FOR EGYPTIAN RELIGIOUS RITES.

Two opposite views have been entertained on the pyramid. While some have imagined its devotion to secret ceremonies in connection with the old faith, others behold in it the negation of belief. Dr. Richardson, the traveller, once exclaimed, " If the temples and tombs are to be considered as remnants of Egyptian idolatry, the pyramids may be regarded as remnants of infidelity." Bishop Russell, the author of an instructive work on Egypt, thought that " it seems reasonable to suppose that all these turnings, apartments, and secrets in architecture were intended for some nobler purpose, and that the Deity rather, which was typified in the outward form of this pile, was to be worshipped within." Norden, in 1737, wrote, " The Egyptian religion was the principal cause of the production of the pyramids."

An older visitor by a century, John Greaves, left this record : " The true reason depends upon higher and more waighty considerations, though I acknowledge those alleaged by Pliny might be secondary motives. And this sprang from the theology of the Ægyptians, who, as Servius shewes in his comment, beleeved that as long as the body endured so long the soule continued with it." A still older English rambler, Sandys, had these reflections when there : " For as a pyramis, beginning at a point, by little and little delateth into all parts, so nature, proceeding from one individual portion (even God, the Sovereign Essence), received diversity of forms, uniting all in the Supreme Head, from whence all excellencies issue." Even Mariette Bey, while opposing the theory of some, affirming that "the pyramids were not monuments of the vain ostentation of kings," sees a religious aspect in the erection; concluding, "they are the impossible obstacles to overturn, and the gigantic proofs of a consoling dogma." He refers to *immortality.*

Mr. Yeates is another viewing the edifice associated with religion, regarding it as an altar. "The summit of the Great Pyramid," says he, "which is by report about sixteen feet square, admits the supposition that here was the high altar, either for sacrifice on any great occasions; or for their chief idol, thereupon placed in former ages." Elsewhere he has it, "Thus does the outward form and appearances of these edifices, duly considered, present to us some idea of the altars and temples of the first ages after the Flood." The tops of Mexican pyramids were certainly used for worship and sacrifices. Bryant, in his great work on mythology, has a similar conception, saying, "They were designed for high altars and temples, and they were constructed in honour of the Deity." He combats the assertion of Herodotus that they were tombs, adding this mean opinion of ancient writers; "they spoke by guess, and I have shown by many instances how usual it was for the Grecians to mistake temples for tombs. If not so," he exclaims, "what occasion was there for a well?"

All this bears upon the Arab tradition, recorded by several writers, that their ancestors used to make pilgrimages to the pyramids, and offer incense to them, sacrificing a black calf. But the religious aspect of the pyramid question cannot be further entered into here.

45. TO CELEBRATE THE MYSTERIES OF LIFE.

All the ancient Pagan mysteries are connected with a sacred vase, a holy bath, a baptismal font, in which the initiated, in a nude state, were completely immersed, and from which they were raised to newness of life. This idea of the regenerating influence of that holy water prevailed alike in the further east and the further west, from the Himalayas across the old continents to Mexico and Peru, or over the Pacific islands. It has literally girdled the earth. We observe it alike in the most ancient as well as most modern forms of heathenism.

According to Prof. Piazzi Smyth the pyramid was erected to preserve the coffer or sarcophagus. According to mystics of various orders a similar opinion has been entertained. Some contend it was to keep inviolate this *symbol of generative life*. It was the cauldron of Ceridwen of the British druids, whence secrets were learned by special and Divine inspiration. It was at once the tomb and the portal to immortality. In a country where, and in an epoch when, certainly, eternity and eternal life occupied more of the popular thought than in any other clime or time, this precious sign of death and life would be watched over with most jealous care.

Recently, a remarkable American work, *Art Magic*, has given a pyramid interpretation. The author speaks of the marvellous box as "a sarcophagus for *living men*, for those initiates who were there taught the solemn problems of life and death, and through the instrumentality of that very coffer attained to that glorious birth of the spirit—that second birth so significantly described." He adds these words, understood in various senses ;—" Slain by violence and laid in the coffer, with him is destroyed the *Master's Word*, on which the building of the Great Temple depends."

It is no wonder that he regards it as "the key-stone of the lost art, which interprets the grand science of living as a Masonic Lodge."

"For ages," says he, "the Great Pyramid has been this rejected stone. The world has not known it, and the builders of science have thrown it away amidst the rubbish of speculative possibilities." Such a man may well term it "a veritable lodge of ancient freemasonry." For this freemasonry Mr. Piazzi Smyth has unnecessarily spoken in terms of contemptuous pity, saying, "Freemasonry, notwithstanding all its boasting, seemed to lead no nearer to a knowledge of the objects and ideas of the coffer than anything connected with the idolatrous religion of the ancient Egyptians."

It was with profound meaning that the anonymous mystic said that "the huge problem of scientific discoveries, the mystic, lidless, wholly unornamented, uninscribed coffer, in the midst of the vast unornamented, uninscribed chamber, was not intended as a model for all generations of succeeding corn and seedsmen, but as a sarcophagus for living men."

Some few thoughtful readers will ponder over these words. There is honey to be got from the lion's mouth, and more than Samson have found it there.

46. A MASONIC HALL.

This view has had many supporters, because the Egyptians were supposed the fathers of freemasonry—the teachings of *Phre*, the solar deity, mason, or raiser of living temples. The pyramid, and prominently the great one, might reasonably have been, with its secret passages, its dark solitudes, its mysterious chambers, regarded as a fitting place for initiation into those sacred mysteries, which were the forerunners of the Eleusinian, &c. All the symbols of the craft are there, and were there, and in the land of Egypt, thousands of years before the masonic temple of Jerusalem was reared by Solomon. It is not wonderful, therefore, that masonic writers, particularly continental and American ones, should have been more drawn to the pyramid than to the Jachin and Boaz of the King of Israel, associated, on Biblical authority, with the two great centres of ancient mysticism, Phœnicia and Egypt.

The Rev. George Oliver, the chief of modern English masonic authors, and a clergyman of the Church of England, must have startled the timid with his idea of the pyramids. "They were, doubtless, erected soon after the Dispersion," he says, "as copies of the great *Phallic* tower, built by Nimrod; and as the latter was designed for initiation, so, also, were the former." Surely some Christian masons would object to a Phallic origin of their craft. But this distinguished masonic authority goes further into the pyramid meaning. He distinctly affirms : "They were intended to contain the apparatus of initiation into the mysteries, and it is highly probable that they were *exclusively* devoted to this important purpose."

As it is intended, hereafter, to treat on Egyptian freemasonry and religion, it is sufficient here to state that one practical difficulty opposes Mr. Oliver's notion of a pyramid being a masonic hall. It is this :—we have clear proofs that immediately upon the finishing of the building every apartment was closed, every passage filled with massive blocks of stone, and the outer entrance effectually concealed. No such pyramid, therefore, could have been an ark of initiation. Neither could it have been, as Bishop Russell and others have thought, a temple for service.

There is a sense, however, wherein it may be said that the pyramid was a masonic edifice, constructed for masonic purposes. But these purposes were higher and nobler than those at present occupying the attention of the Order.

47. SPECIAL REVELATIONS TO MYSTICS.

In a general way it may be said that the pyramid has special revelations of a mysterious character. The ordinary man of fair education and common sense would, as a rule, see nothing more mysterious in it than in the Royal Exchange. It would for him have nothing special to tell of an outside character. He might, perhaps, marvel at the stupidity of wasting so much time and money on so practically useless a building. In the whole he would recognise a tomb, and nothing more. It would suggest as much to him as " the primrose by the river's brink " to Wordsworth's countryman.

It may be further said that such a man, if looking into this little volume, might possibly have a pitying sneer or smile for the reader of what would appear to him such baseless mathematical and scientific calculations, as connected with the pyramid. He would naturally look upon Dufeu, Hekekyan Bey, Agnew, Piazzi Smyth, John Taylor, Wild, John Wilson, and the like, as sheer dreamers.

One must rejoice, nevertheless, that there are those who look beneath the surface of things, and dig for hidden treasure. In spite of the *pooh-poohings* of men who are ever preaching about

"Facts—plain facts, sir," there really are strange revelations from the pyramid which are recognised by thoughtful, sober citizens of the world. An increasing number are beginning to ask, with the Rosicrucian :—

"Is it reasonable to conclude, at a period when knowledge was at the highest, and when human powers were, in comparison with ours at the present time, prodigious, that all these indescribable physical efforts, such gigantic achievements as those of the Egyptians, were devoted to a mistake? that the myriads of the Nile were fools, labouring in the dark?"

But there is another class, more truly mystic than any we have mentioned, whose notions, if revealed privately to the expounders of millennial markings in the pyramid, would extort derision and contumely, but who are nevertheless worthy of a word in a book on the "Why?" of the pyramid.

Still, as these mystics write not for the public, have no mission to fulfil for the public, and care not one straw for the public, it seems hardly worth while to say anything about them to the public.

It has been the writer's good fortune to come across the path of one or two such persons. Perhaps other men, in a pilgrimage of sixty years, who have good faith in their fellow-creatures' intelligence, and sympathy with honest, earnest aspirations, encounter some who seem but to live on the confines of this everyday world of ours. The dreamers are seen to have some method in their supposed madness, and some reason in their wild imaginings. In these cases, an incoherent speech testifies to the dread of ridicule, the consciousness of being misunderstood, or the conviction that the truth is too sacred for utterance.

M. Caviglia, born in Malta, dying in Paris at the age of
seventy-four, in 1845, buried with his Bible beside him, was one
of these mystics, and so passionately devoted to pyramid study
that for some time he lived in an apartment—Mr. Piazzi
Smyth's symbol of heaven—over the King's Chamber.

Lord Lindsay met him at Gizeh, admired and honoured him.
He was, as he himself expressed it, "*tout à fait pyramidale.*"
His lordship wrote, "We are told that in Ceylon there are
insects that take the shape and colour of the branch or leaf they
feed upon; Caviglia seems to partake of their nature, he is
really assimilating to a pyramid." This was not said in ridicule.
He described him as "happy with his pyramid, his mysticism,
and his Bible." Even then, at sixty-six years of age, he had,
we are told, "reared a pyramid of the most extraordinary
mysticism—astrology, magnetism, magic (his favourite studies),
its corner-stones; while on each face of the airy vision he sees
inscribed, in letters of light, invisible to all but himself, eluci-
datory texts of Scripture."

Mr. Ramsay has this account:—"He has strange, unearthly
ideas, which seem to open up to you, as he says them, whole
vistas of unheard-of ground, which close up again as suddenly,
so that one can hardly know what his theories are. He says, it
would be highly dangerous to communicate them, and looks
mystical."

One who knew something about *Lost Secrets* wrote thus of
him :—" By studying the remains of Pagan antiquity in the only
way they can be profitably studied, namely, through the medium
of the occult sciences, Caviglia had discovered the long-lost secret
of the pyramids. And with the discovery of the central mystery

of Egyptian paganism the great central truth of Christianity, historically considered, had revealed itself to him."

One who studied such questions for half a century, and who lately left this Babel of ours for the " dimly-shadowed shore," told the writer that there were untold secrets of value in the Great Pyramid, and that the pyramid builders possessed the secret of all philosophical mysticism on the basis of astronomical fact.

There is something in the pyramid; and men who see what others cannot, would not, see, if derided for their second sight, may yet be proved to have a vision true and clear.

The enthusiastic French *savant*, M. Dufeu, proudly affirms that "not a stone has been set, not a dimension has been determined, which may not have its reason why, and concurred to establish scientific formulæ to represent, and eternally to preserve, the previous knowledge acquired by the immortal architects who erected these colossal masses."

He, like some others, while maintaining that "only a part of the veil has been raised which hid the high destination of pyramids," can indulge glowing expectations of new revelations.

"Who knows," cries he, "what treasure may yet burst forth from the secular flanks of these great constructions, whose incontestable utility and importance will be no more denied by any one. New discoveries, encircling with a fresh aureola the head of the eminent learned of a pre-historic epoch, will impose on us an addition to our admiration of their vast genius."

THE END.

A CATALOG OF SELECTED
DOVER BOOKS
IN ALL FIELDS OF INTEREST

A CATALOG OF SELECTED DOVER
BOOKS IN ALL FIELDS OF INTEREST

CONCERNING THE SPIRITUAL IN ART, Wassily Kandinsky. Pioneering work by father of abstract art. Thoughts on color theory, nature of art. Analysis of earlier masters. 12 illustrations. 80pp. of text. 5⅜ x 8½.   23411-8

ANIMALS: 1,419 Copyright-Free Illustrations of Mammals, Birds, Fish, Insects, etc., Jim Harter (ed.). Clear wood engravings present, in extremely lifelike poses, over 1,000 species of animals. One of the most extensive pictorial sourcebooks of its kind. Captions. Index. 284pp. 9 x 12.   23766-4

CELTIC ART: The Methods of Construction, George Bain. Simple geometric techniques for making Celtic interlacements, spirals, Kells-type initials, animals, humans, etc. Over 500 illustrations. 160pp. 9 x 12. (Available in U.S. only.)   22923-8

AN ATLAS OF ANATOMY FOR ARTISTS, Fritz Schider. Most thorough reference work on art anatomy in the world. Hundreds of illustrations, including selections from works by Vesalius, Leonardo, Goya, Ingres, Michelangelo, others. 593 illustrations. 192pp. 7⅛ x 10¼.   20241-0

CELTIC HAND STROKE-BY-STROKE (Irish Half-Uncial from "The Book of Kells"): An Arthur Baker Calligraphy Manual, Arthur Baker. Complete guide to creating each letter of the alphabet in distinctive Celtic manner. Covers hand position, strokes, pens, inks, paper, more. Illustrated. 48pp. 8¼ x 11.   24336-2

EASY ORIGAMI, John Montroll. Charming collection of 32 projects (hat, cup, pelican, piano, swan, many more) specially designed for the novice origami hobbyist. Clearly illustrated easy-to-follow instructions insure that even beginning papercrafters will achieve successful results. 48pp. 8¼ x 11.   27298-2

THE COMPLETE BOOK OF BIRDHOUSE CONSTRUCTION FOR WOOD-WORKERS, Scott D. Campbell. Detailed instructions, illustrations, tables. Also data on bird habitat and instinct patterns. Bibliography. 3 tables. 63 illustrations in 15 figures. 48pp. 5¼ x 8½.   24407-5

BLOOMINGDALE'S ILLUSTRATED 1886 CATALOG: Fashions, Dry Goods and Housewares, Bloomingdale Brothers. Famed merchants' extremely rare catalog depicting about 1,700 products: clothing, housewares, firearms, dry goods, jewelry, more. Invaluable for dating, identifying vintage items. Also, copyright-free graphics for artists, designers. Co-published with Henry Ford Museum & Greenfield Village. 160pp. 8¼ x 11.   25780-0

HISTORIC COSTUME IN PICTURES, Braun & Schneider. Over 1,450 costumed figures in clearly detailed engravings–from dawn of civilization to end of 19th century. Captions. Many folk costumes. 256pp. 8⅜ x 11¾.   23150-X

STICKLEY CRAFTSMAN FURNITURE CATALOGS, Gustav Stickley and L. & J. G. Stickley. Beautiful, functional furniture in two authentic catalogs from 1910. 594 illustrations, including 277 photos, show settles, rockers, armchairs, reclining chairs, bookcases, desks, tables. 183pp. 6½ x 9¼.   23838-5

AMERICAN LOCOMOTIVES IN HISTORIC PHOTOGRAPHS: 1858 to 1949, Ron Ziel (ed.). A rare collection of 126 meticulously detailed official photographs, called "builder portraits," of American locomotives that majestically chronicle the rise of steam locomotive power in America. Introduction. Detailed captions. xi+ 129pp. 9 x 12.   27393-8

AMERICA'S LIGHTHOUSES: An Illustrated History, Francis Ross Holland, Jr. Delightfully written, profusely illustrated fact-filled survey of over 200 American light-houses since 1716. History, anecdotes, technological advances, more. 240pp. 8 x 10¾.
25576-X

TOWARDS A NEW ARCHITECTURE, Le Corbusier. Pioneering manifesto by founder of "International School." Technical and aesthetic theories, views of industry, economics, relation of form to function, "mass-production split" and much more. Profusely illustrated. 320pp. 6⅛ x 9¼. (Available in U.S. only.)   25023-7

HOW THE OTHER HALF LIVES, Jacob Riis. Famous journalistic record, exposing poverty and degradation of New York slums around 1900, by major social reformer. 100 striking and influential photographs. 233pp. 10 x 7⅞.   22012-5

FRUIT KEY AND TWIG KEY TO TREES AND SHRUBS, William M. Harlow. One of the handiest and most widely used identification aids. Fruit key covers 120 deciduous and evergreen species; twig key 160 deciduous species. Easily used. Over 300 photographs. 126pp. 5⅜ x 8½.   20511-8

COMMON BIRD SONGS, Dr. Donald J. Borror. Songs of 60 most common U.S. birds: robins, sparrows, cardinals, bluejays, finches, more—arranged in order of increasing complexity. Up to 9 variations of songs of each species.
Cassette and manual 99911-4

ORCHIDS AS HOUSE PLANTS, Rebecca Tyson Northen. Grow cattleyas and many other kinds of orchids—in a window, in a case, or under artificial light. 63 illustrations. 148pp. 5⅜ x 8½.   23261-1

MONSTER MAZES, Dave Phillips. Masterful mazes at four levels of difficulty. Avoid deadly perils and evil creatures to find magical treasures. Solutions for all 32 exciting illustrated puzzles. 48pp. 8¼ x 11.   26005-4

MOZART'S DON GIOVANNI (DOVER OPERA LIBRETTO SERIES), Wolfgang Amadeus Mozart. Introduced and translated by Ellen H. Bleiler. Standard Italian libretto, with complete English translation. Convenient and thoroughly portable—an ideal companion for reading along with a recording or the performance itself. Introduction. List of characters. Plot summary. 121pp. 5¼ x 8½.   24944-1

TECHNICAL MANUAL AND DICTIONARY OF CLASSICAL BALLET, Gail Grant. Defines, explains, comments on steps, movements, poses and concepts. 15-page pictorial section. Basic book for student, viewer. 127pp. 5⅜ x 8½.   21843-0

THE CLARINET AND CLARINET PLAYING, David Pino. Lively, comprehensive work features suggestions about technique, musicianship, and musical interpretation, as well as guidelines for teaching, making your own reeds, and preparing for public performance. Includes an intriguing look at clarinet history. "A godsend," *The Clarinet,* Journal of the International Clarinet Society. Appendixes. 7 illus. 320pp. 5⅜ x 8½. 40270-3

HOLLYWOOD GLAMOR PORTRAITS, John Kobal (ed.). 145 photos from 1926-49. Harlow, Gable, Bogart, Bacall; 94 stars in all. Full background on photographers, technical aspects. 160pp. 8⅜ x 11¼. 23352-9

THE ANNOTATED CASEY AT THE BAT: A Collection of Ballads about the Mighty Casey/Third, Revised Edition, Martin Gardner (ed.). Amusing sequels and parodies of one of America's best-loved poems: Casey's Revenge, Why Casey Whiffed, Casey's Sister at the Bat, others. 256pp. 5⅜ x 8½. 28598-7

THE RAVEN AND OTHER FAVORITE POEMS, Edgar Allan Poe. Over 40 of the author's most memorable poems: "The Bells," "Ulalume," "Israfel," "To Helen," "The Conqueror Worm," "Eldorado," "Annabel Lee," many more. Alphabetic lists of titles and first lines. 64pp. 5$^{3}/_{16}$ x 8¼. 26685-0

PERSONAL MEMOIRS OF U. S. GRANT, Ulysses Simpson Grant. Intelligent, deeply moving firsthand account of Civil War campaigns, considered by many the finest military memoirs ever written. Includes letters, historic photographs, maps and more. 528pp. 6⅛ x 9¼. 28587-1

ANCIENT EGYPTIAN MATERIALS AND INDUSTRIES, A. Lucas and J. Harris. Fascinating, comprehensive, thoroughly documented text describes this ancient civilization's vast resources and the processes that incorporated them in daily life, including the use of animal products, building materials, cosmetics, perfumes and incense, fibers, glazed ware, glass and its manufacture, materials used in the mummification process, and much more. 544pp. 6⅛ x 9¼. (Available in U.S. only.) 40446-3

RUSSIAN STORIES/RUSSKIE RASSKAZY: A Dual-Language Book, edited by Gleb Struve. Twelve tales by such masters as Chekhov, Tolstoy, Dostoevsky, Pushkin, others. Excellent word-for-word English translations on facing pages, plus teaching and study aids, Russian/English vocabulary, biographical/critical introductions, more. 416pp. 5⅜ x 8½. 26244-8

PHILADELPHIA THEN AND NOW: 60 Sites Photographed in the Past and Present, Kenneth Finkel and Susan Oyama. Rare photographs of City Hall, Logan Square, Independence Hall, Betsy Ross House, other landmarks juxtaposed with contemporary views. Captures changing face of historic city. Introduction. Captions. 128pp. 8¼ x 11. 25790-8

AIA ARCHITECTURAL GUIDE TO NASSAU AND SUFFOLK COUNTIES, LONG ISLAND, The American Institute of Architects, Long Island Chapter, and the Society for the Preservation of Long Island Antiquities. Comprehensive, well-researched and generously illustrated volume brings to life over three centuries of Long Island's great architectural heritage. More than 240 photographs with authoritative, extensively detailed captions. 176pp. 8¼ x 11. 26946-9

NORTH AMERICAN INDIAN LIFE: Customs and Traditions of 23 Tribes, Elsie Clews Parsons (ed.). 27 fictionalized essays by noted anthropologists examine religion, customs, government, additional facets of life among the Winnebago, Crow, Zuni, Eskimo, other tribes. 480pp. 6⅛ x 9¼. 27377-6

THE STORY OF THE TITANIC AS TOLD BY ITS SURVIVORS, Jack Winocour (ed.). What it was really like. Panic, despair, shocking inefficiency, and a little heroism. More thrilling than any fictional account. 26 illustrations. 320pp. 5⅜ x 8½. 20610-6

FAIRY AND FOLK TALES OF THE IRISH PEASANTRY, William Butler Yeats (ed.). Treasury of 64 tales from the twilight world of Celtic myth and legend: "The Soul Cages," "The Kildare Pooka," "King O'Toole and his Goose," many more. Introduction and Notes by W. B. Yeats. 352pp. 5⅜ x 8½. 26941-8

BUDDHIST MAHAYANA TEXTS, E. B. Cowell and others (eds.). Superb, accurate translations of basic documents in Mahayana Buddhism, highly important in history of religions. The Buddha-karita of Asvaghosha, Larger Sukhavativyuha, more. 448pp. 5⅜ x 8½. 25552-2

ONE TWO THREE . . . INFINITY: Facts and Speculations of Science, George Gamow. Great physicist's fascinating, readable overview of contemporary science: number theory, relativity, fourth dimension, entropy, genes, atomic structure, much more. 128 illustrations. Index. 352pp. 5⅜ x 8½. 25664-2

EXPERIMENTATION AND MEASUREMENT, W. J. Youden. Introductory manual explains laws of measurement in simple terms and offers tips for achieving accuracy and minimizing errors. Mathematics of measurement, use of instruments, experimenting with machines. 1994 edition. Foreword. Preface. Introduction. Epilogue. Selected Readings. Glossary. Index. Tables and figures. 128pp. 5⅜ x 8½. 40451-X

DALÍ ON MODERN ART: The Cuckolds of Antiquated Modern Art, Salvador Dalí. Influential painter skewers modern art and its practitioners. Outrageous evaluations of Picasso, Cézanne, Turner, more. 15 renderings of paintings discussed. 44 calligraphic decorations by Dalí. 96pp. 5⅜ x 8½. (Available in U.S. only.) 29220-7

ANTIQUE PLAYING CARDS: A Pictorial History, Henry René D'Allemagne. Over 900 elaborate, decorative images from rare playing cards (14th–20th centuries): Bacchus, death, dancing dogs, hunting scenes, royal coats of arms, players cheating, much more. 96pp. 9¼ x 12¼. 29265-7

MAKING FURNITURE MASTERPIECES: 30 Projects with Measured Drawings, Franklin H. Gottshall. Step-by-step instructions, illustrations for constructing handsome, useful pieces, among them a Sheraton desk, Chippendale chair, Spanish desk, Queen Anne table and a William and Mary dressing mirror. 224pp. 8⅛ x 11¼. 29338-6

THE FOSSIL BOOK: A Record of Prehistoric Life, Patricia V. Rich et al. Profusely illustrated definitive guide covers everything from single-celled organisms and dinosaurs to birds and mammals and the interplay between climate and man. Over 1,500 illustrations. 760pp. 7½ x 10⅛. 29371-8

Paperbound unless otherwise indicated. Available at your book dealer, online at **www.doverpublications.com**, or by writing to Dept. GI, Dover Publications, Inc., 31 East 2nd Street, Mineola, NY 11501. For current price information or for free catalogues (please indicate field of interest), write to Dover Publications or log on to **www.doverpublications.com** and see every Dover book in print. Dover publishes more than 500 books each year on science, elementary and advanced mathematics, biology, music, art, literary history, social sciences, and other areas.